TIME IS

RUNNING

OUT

Now Is The Time to Honor

Your Journey on Mother

Earth

Darlene,
Many Blessings &
Light to you

Crystal Gingras

CRYSTAL D. GINGRAS

Dedication

To Mother Earth

You are here for all of us.

You always have been and always will.

You are as evident as the shining stars in the night sky.

You are the pounding in my heart;

The waves of everlasting emotions that fill me.

You filter me.

You ground me to my core.

You are my inner strength;

My inner wisdom;

You are life.

From you,

From ground,

From the womb of my beautiful mother,

Sue Morningstar, thank you.

Crystal D. Gingras, November 2007, Guatemala

TABLE OF CONTENTS

ACKNOWLEDGMENTS

I want to thank my great grandfather, Chief Shunatona, who guides me and reminds me to laugh freely open-heartedly. To all the people who shared with my heart, I thank you and I am grateful for growth in this lifetime: My mother Sue Shunatona, my father Donald Dale Gingras, my sister Eva Shunatona, and my two brothers Nesahdo J.R. Shunatona, and Jason Shunatona-Forsberg. There are so many special friends, ancestors, teachers and family in my life and other dimensions and I am so grateful for each and every one of you. Thank you Dwight E. Roth for your assistance in editing this book and inspiring me to finish writing. Special thanks to Mallory Chamberlin for editing my book and Most of all, I want to thank Mother Earth for supporting all of us here and the Creator for putting us all here with each other for love and support. Life is truly a blessing, and I appreciate being able to experience all of its beauty. I am forever grateful.

With all the love in my heart,

Crystal Donielle Gingras

CHAPTER ONE

₪ Messages from Mother Earth

"Here is my story from my heart and spirit, to yours."

~ Crystal D. Gingras ~

I attended a vision quest ceremony in 2009, where I fasted for three days without food or water and slept as little as possible (we are supposed to stay awake the entire time). My purpose was to pray for a vision to see what I needed to elaborate on in my life in the future. This was not the first time I had practiced this particular ceremony. I had completed my first vision quest about five years before.

My first vision quest only lasted for a single night, then I was called back in the morning after sunrise. Before I went to be alone with the earth that night to pray, everyone who was present in the seven days of ceremonies cleansed off in the sacred lodge with the stone people and the water for cleansing.

Upon my return of the ceremony through the night, I went back inside of the lodge to cleanse again, and share my vision if I wanted with the elder who was conducting the ceremony. I had decided earlier that day to sit on a tree that had fallen over near a stream of water before I went into sweat lodge. I had to cross over the water to get there, and by the time that the sweat lodge was over, it was dark, so I had to remember how to get there. I used a walking stick to go through the stream of water and find my special place to sit through the night. When I arrived, I sat on the large old fallen tree that I found earlier in the daylight and began to look around at my surroundings in the dark night.

It was very quiet, dark, and scary for some time. There were others who were afraid to stay outside all night, so there were only a few of us doing our vision out of the group. After what seemed like several hours passed by, I began looking for the sun to rise from the east. The time went be very slowly and it was beginning to get very cold. If felt as if an entire night and half a day went by, and I still couldn't see the sun rising. I was looking up into the sky when all of a sudden something very large yet quiet flew by and splashed drops of water all over me. I felt something starring right into my soul and when I slowly turned to my right, there on a branch sticking up from the log beside me, was an owl starring right back at me. The only way to express how I felt in words was "whoa". Not too long after we looked at each other in the eyes, the sun started to rise and the owl flew away into the morning sky. Shortly after, I was called back to the sweat lodge by a loud calling noise. I decided to keep my experience to myself that morning...

A vision or experience that happens to you during a vision quest is not something that you typically share with anyone right away (except for the person looking after you that is leading the ceremony). You are usually told that it is up to you to share what you have seen, but some actually require that you share what you have seen or experienced with them. A vision is to be held very sacred and private to yourself or with your personal family. It is good to hold onto your visions for at least a week, if not longer before you share them with others. I was taught this way in order for you to have time to soak in the energy and powers of your vision and understand their full meaning. Sometimes, explanations and realizations of your visions will not be understood for years. They will appear when the time is right for you and meant to be understood.

Not only what you see in a vision quest will reveal things that you need to see, but everything that actually takes place and happens during that time period is important to notice. When you go on a vision quest, or other ceremonies, you will have an officiator, supporters/ grounders, and protectors/tools. Supporters will be people present other than the person leading that will be holding space for you while you are praying. Those people are present to give you the extra energy and grounding that you need. Your protectors and tools will be your sacred pipe, an eagle feather or hawk feather and some sage and tobacco. This ceremony is practiced in a couple various ways depending on who is leading the ceremony and watching over you.

The week of my three day vision quest, I had asked someone to be my supporter for me and he said yes. I told them that I was praying for a vision and that I needed someone to be there for me while I was out praying for a few days. I was all packed up the morning of the trip and went and picked him up to ride with me. We drove hours to the vision quest site, and when we arrived it was still the middle of the day. My supporter and I set up the tent that he was staying in. The leader was being picked up at an airport about two hours away. By the early evening, it was starting to become extremely cold and windy. I remember the car they arrived in had a broken window and they were freezing all the way there. Our teacher had to go sit by the fire right away and warm up.

As instructed by the leader when he arrived, I was praying and getting my sacred pipe filled with tobacco to take with me on my journey. I was all ready to go into sweat lodge and prepare, and then something unexpected happened. My supporter was scared, cold, and wanted to leave and go home very bad. After an hour of talking to him and the leader, we decided the best thing to do was to let him drive my car home. He agreed and left right away, and I stayed to continue on my quest. This was something very important for me to notice pending my time there.

On the last day of my fast, I saw myself participating in a sweat lodge ceremony with respected elders from different nations. I saw someone from Asia, Africa, India and a few other places. I also saw many round looking figures spread throughout the cities in people's yards, which I thought were sweat lodges at the time (sweat lodges are made from small willow tree branches bent into a particular shape and size, low to the ground. Outside of the lodges are fire pits where the fire heats up the rocks to help the people inside to sweat away any old useless junk no longer needed on their journey in this lifetime. The sweat lodge ceremony is practiced all over the world for many, many years, and I have been attending since I was one years old).

Shortly after I saw a couple visions, someone came near my sacred space and told me that it was time to come back. As I was walking back towards the sweat lodge, someone was calling my name. There was someone that was hurting from sitting for days that needed my assistance. This was second thing that I noticed while on my vision quest. So, I helped out that person to regain some strength. Not one second after I sat down, another person was in pain and needed my assistance. After wards, we all made it into the lodge, and there were people that were practically crying from their physical pain. We had a child present at the time, and the leader felt that it was important to stay strong for them. This was the third lesson that I noticed from this ceremony.

After the sweat lodge was finished, it was time for us to feast together to end the ceremony. I called one of my spirit sisters, Ju-Lynda, back in Wichita to pick me up from ceremony. Her and her father came and picked me up from ceremony. When I arrived back home to the contemporary world in Wichita, KS from this ceremony, I did what every present person would do… I checked my email. There was one in particular that stood out. It was from a man in California about building natural earth-ship homes on the reservation in Pine Ridge, S.D. When I opened his email and saw the pictures of the round houses on his email, this is what I believed I was meant to be doing next. I had heard about natural housing before and have always had an interest in learning more and I definitely had an interest in following my vision and helping out the indigenous people of this land. Although it was rather late at night, I called him right away and shared with him the vision I had in ceremony. That next day, I made plans to travel to Pine Ridge and help out with building the natural earth ship home. Although these ceremonies and short trips helping out are very important to do, I know there is so much more than we can all do to reach out to others.

Humanity has poisoned the earth, the water, and, therefore, the air, the clouds, and all of life. We have ripped her veins (trees) into shreds over and over again, we trample on her and drench her with chemicals every day, and we continue without hesitation. Although the trees can drink fresh water that has been cleansed deep within the earth, many humans do not collect their water from that deep within the earth. There are many different programs set in place that help to clean out the water and the earth, but it takes many years and lots of time and money. Thousands of dumping and spilling of chemicals have occurred all over the United States and all over the globe. Although there are thousands of people working with the water filtration systems worldwide, there is still a grave need for assistance from humanity to maintain the water.

People keep nagging about needing more material rewards and a larger industrial world, yet so many are struggling to survive and feel alone. It seems as if people are selfishly concentrating on changing themselves just to feel loved and accepted by others. In the meantime, we are forgetting about honoring and loving the world and the elements that sustain us and fulfill our wants. The earth and the elements are often a reflection of how we are all treating each other and feeling on the inside. Are you aware of the soil and water chemical levels in your own state? Are you aware of how many years your city plans to take action to clean the water out there?

With all of the wars, murders, rapes, and deaths over thousands of years, we are left with wounded hearts, distressed spirits, and lost souls. Although I do not concentrate on the dark part of life, it is important to acknowledge that without it, we would not be here on this planet. Many seeds of "evil" touched the lives of millions in all cultures all over the world, but also many seeds of light balanced and cleared the burdens of the past, so that we can all move forward. Because of the pain that has happened to millions over the years, there are many children and adults who are hindered and paralyzed in this pain. Many children, men, and women suffer from long-life addictions and illnesses who take medications. We are here to learn and grow together and offer a helping hand when someone is reaching out.

In order to do a small part to help the children of Mother Earth, I wrote this book to help get the message to those who need to hear it. She wants us to learn to live in a more balanced way and know that we have power to cleanse and balance the water, the earth, and all the elements by healing ourselves. Besides speaking to children in schools, and groups of adults in different states, I love traveling to ceremonies and sharing what I can at that time. Sometimes it's singing and drumming, doing massage and energy work, or I have even offered Oneness Blessings in San Jose. There are many different gifts that we all carry, and being able to share them with others is a blessing.

I visited Pine Ridge again the next year, except I went to another place nearby in Nebraska. While I was there, I heard some of the elders talk about all the deaths that resulted from chemicals in the water and the land. I saw the scars from flesh-eating rot that was on a woman's body before she healed herself with plants in her garden.

I went there to help build natural housing and assist with permaculture (which is all natural gardening and farming of the land). When I arrived at a house to ask a family there if they were interested in natural housing (earth ship homes from dirt and recycled tires), the children scurried inside shouting there was a white person there. I cried when I left from the children's reaction, and I cried when I heard the story of how they have been trained in school for many years. They were taught to run and hide because they have been massacred for so many years, even in my time.

A journalist that was born in Pine Ridge shared how the children were taught to hide under beds and to duck underneath windows if there was ever gunfire. She also shared her personal stories of being chemically poisoned by the water and having to cure her flesh- eating rot with herbs from her garden. She showed me the scars covering the back of her legs and her garden where she grows natural medicinal plants that she eats. She currently resides alone on a reservation in South Dakota.

In 2008, while I was traveling around South Dakota, and I heard about an Indian reservation where they shut off the electricity in severe cold weather even when children and elderly in wheelchairs were in the homes. I personally witnessed the mold and holes in ceilings of the trailers that are on the reservations. There was no running water on the inside of the house and they still used an outhouse. Their dinner was water and meat in a huge pot and I was honored the elder invited me to supper. The water is not safe to drink anymore in so many different places. Including Pawnee, my reservation where I lived in Oklahoma in 2010.

On the reservations that I have visited over the years, there is a very high rate of suicide in teenagers, and the drug and alcohol rates are very great. I heard about South Dakota, being like a third-world country, and although it's not as bad, there is still a need for balance in that state. There are many churches and groups who may assist for a week or two, but permanent people and businesses are needed to make a lasting difference. The job rates are low on some reservations, and in Pine Ridge, there is hardly any fresh produce; it is difficult to grow crops as the grasshoppers will eat the food as soon as it grows. It is useful to build fences around the crops and gardens and get birds to eat as many grasshoppers as possible. You can drive through the reservation and see all of the dead trees, empty land with no grocery stores or health and rehab centers. They do have a new school, and nearby there are huge painted signs warning to stay off of drugs.

When I visited Montana a few years earlier in 2005 to meet my father, I saw how bad the drug problems are there too. I have only been to about ten or fifteen different reservations, but I have watched documentaries and videos on many more. I also met a lot of other indigenous people from different Nations than I when I was on The Longest Walk II to save Mother Earth. I housed the people that were on the Walk in Wichita, KS at the Riverview Retreat Center that I managed for a couple of years. The owner, Richard has been like a father to me for many years since I started attending ceremonies on his land as a child. While I was managing there, I found out about the 30th Commemorative from The Walk from Alcatraz in California all the way to Washington D.C. I thought that this was an important walk, as we were walking to respect and honor the land, each other, the water and all of life. They stayed at the Retreat Center for about a week and then moved on towards Washington D.C. About one month later I met up with them in Pennsylvania and walked with the group the rest of the way to Washington D.C. on July 11th 2008.

Some of the things that we concentrated on were getting families and tribes back their remains and sacred objects that are on display in museums. I remember seeing a Pawnee sacred pipe on display where I went to school and wondering why it wasn't on our tribal lands. I heard about my Ponca sister's ancestor's clothes being on display at museums in D.C. and there are so many more stories that all the people had to share. We also concentrated on ski resorts that wanted to expand which would kill lots of forestry, animals, and harm a nearby tribal members. There were many voices that wanted to be heard on this sacred walk.

Some of the concerns that were shared with me were, "We must befriend the ground of the earth once again."… "I am learning about the groundwater that is almost depleted in Black Mesa, the only water source for the Navajo people since they don't have rights to the water from the Colorado River." Another person says, "The Mojave tribe is facing ground water contamination issues with chromium (and that is only what they know for sure) which I will move into the Colorado River, and the California energy companies building huge facilities and desecrating places of prayer, burial, and medicine." And of the least messages that I have written down from someone is, "There are lime issues near/in the Colorado that the Hualapai people (and more) are currently being affected by." I typed and shared this information with all the people that I could in Wichita during their stay with us from April 16th-April 18th 2008.

There were many supporters in Wichita, KS. A lot of close friends and family came out to the Indian Center to help support while they were here. One of the strongest memories that I have is when we were walking towards Newton with the staffs down north Broadway and a little boy at an elementary school across the street drops down to his knees and puts his hands together to pray. He had to have been about only five or six years old. There was also a very young man from Japan who walked with us who played the drum and sang a chant every day. And when he came to the retreat, he loved to lie on the huge cypress tree table that Richard had in the solarium. There were war veterans and elders who had walked on this Journey thirty years ago. I was honored to offer my assistance and humbled to join the walk. There were a couple of families with children as well as single mothers with children. The children were such a blessing to have on the walk and carried small staffs and hand held sticks. I have many, many memories from this walk, filled with happiness, strength, and lots of pain, sadness and heartbreak.

While we were all camping in D.C., we were each asked to write a manifesto. The question that they asked us was, "Why have you come on The Longest Walk II: Northern Route, as it relates to its purpose?" I wrote, (I will do my best to write all that I wrote, as my paper has something spilled all over it) "To recognize and support the message that the Longest Walk II carries across the lands of our Mother Earth. I am here for all the children and for the many generations to come. I walk for peace, harmony, wisdom, and for all of the promises and words that were spoken to my Relatives, Ancestors, and Elders to be fulfilled. Most of all, to give hope to our children."

"I have come on the Longest Walk II out of respect and honor to the people of all of life. I walk for the indigenous peoples and for my ancestors. This walk is a part of the Red Road that I follow and I will continue to follow; to protect and to pass on the traditional ways of my people for many generations to follow."

The next question they asked was, "What issues relating to the Walk are of greatest concern to you?" My response, "There are many issues that concern me, including the traditions of the indigenous peoples being passed on to the children. Also, a concern of mine is the return of sacred objects and remains to free our ancestors and pass on the ways of the people. Most importantly, the land, the water, and animal life that feed us, clothe us, and support us."

"The greatest concern to me is the way the message of the

Longest Walk II is carried to the people. It is important to recognize and honor the staffs and this journey as a ceremony in a traditional way, so that our children will learn and remember this Walk in a Good Way."

The third question they asked, "What thoughts do you have on indigenous peoples issues related to sovereignty and self determination?" My response was, "First, we have to be free on the land that was stolen and the waters need to be freed for our people. The wild-life has been destroyed; being sold for home-fronts and hunting grounds. The land and all life is being disrespected and destroyed. The pain of our lands, ancestors, waters, trees, and animals being taken away and destroyed are causing us to suffer great pain, turning to alcohol and drugs, and hard to find tradition, hard to find our voice in the White Man's World. We need to each take action for our families. Take a stand for yourself and learn your traditions and the ways and the truths of your people and where they came from (to the best of their knowledge). To understand your rights and understand what you can do for the indigenous peoples is the first step to make a difference for preserving all walks of life and this Mother Earth.

Last question I was asked in D.C., "What actions should arise of this Walk?" I can only speak for myself and my own actions. I made a vow to the Creator to Walk the Red Road. To help in the way the Creator has sent me. To be there when needed; to offer my hands and my life to carry on this prayer for our people each day I'm blessed with life."

"All indigenous peoples involved and their children will become a message for their relatives, for their people back home and improve their awareness of traditions and the importance of preserving Mother Earth and all life. Also, become more involved within the indigenous communities to continue to support and protect sacred sites and return stolen traditions from museums to the people and ancestors where they rightfully belong."

This was a huge eye opener for me to meet and see many different tribes and learn about all of the struggles that they are going through. Some of the women never spoke and walked with their eyes down towards the ground. Many people did not want to take any pictures and stayed away from news reporters and people trying to make movies.

Seeing all of these families and children without electricity, running water in the house, healthy foods, or inside bathrooms, made me wonder where are all of our leaders? What are they doing, and why can't they help these children? Why do I see thousands of people traveling to other countries, when we need just hundreds to help in this country? I believe in helping out other countries as we are all important, but why are the children of this country not on the news and receiving more assistance? This book and the profits of this book are for the children of mother earth, starting with all of those left behind and forgotten.

Mother Earth says, "*You are not alone. I am here, right under your every step, right here every time you walk, drive, ride your bike; I am beneath you holding you up; I am carefully watching over you no matter what you do or say to me, because I love you unconditionally. I am the earth mother. I am your mother and each and every one of you is my child. You are forgiven every day that you walk this earth because I am here to cleanse you and wipe your tears. I am here to feed you food from my womb, and give you water from my streams, and from my very veins that run through my body. You are never alone, for I am always here. Your brothers and sisters are the trees. You carry the same DNA. Just because you don't look alike or move alike does not mean that you are not related. Your brothers and sisters are here to help carry your spirit; to give you medicine when you are sick; to give breath when you can't breathe; and help you when you feel like you cannot go on alone. Your time on earth is running out. You can only help yourself and you have everything you need right where you are. You have the earth right under your feet, and you have the sky right above you and the waters all around you. You do not have to give up. This is not a demand, but a choice that you have to make. All decisions are all up to you."*

Here are some questions to ask yourself when you are ready to take a real look at where you are on your path today. Some of these questions you can answer in your mind, and some of them you might want to write down and take time to meditate on the question and write down your answer. If you have a journal that you write in, the questions in this book will be suitable for self-growth and understanding. Remember always to write down the first thing that comes to mind, even if it does not make sense at the time. Learning to trust your intuition is a part of learning where you are in life and with practice, this becomes easier.

Answer These Questions

How do you want to live your life from now on?

_____

_____

_____

_____

Do you want to travel the world and experience different cultures and life?

_____

_____

_____

_____

Are you concerned with your health and want more energy?

_____

_____

_____

_____

What is it exactly that you feel is necessary to live a fulfilled life?

_____

_____

_____

Do you want to say, "Today is a good day to live, or today is a good day to die"?

_____

_____

_____

_____

Are you satisfied with your accomplishments and ready to *take the journey* if today was your last day?

_____

_____

_____

_____

Or, are you sick and tired of the same old routine and want a new beginning?

_____

_____

_____

_____

What are the changes that you can start making today?

_____

_____

_____

_____

What does your heart say that it really wants to accomplish in this lifetime?

_____

_____

_____

_____

Just for a moment, close your eyes and ask your heart what it really yearns for right now. Maybe your heart is sad and lonely. What does your heart look like when you close your eyes and focus your attention within your heart space? Maybe you need some clearing, and your heart area needs to be cleaned up and nurtured. Take some time to clean out any clutter that may be there by imaging you are sweeping or washing your heart with some warm water. If your heart center feels sad and lonely, then imagine placing some flowers at your heart and then actually get yourself some flowers to place next to your bed, or in your home. Take time to nurture your heart; it is the center of your existence.

List all of your current fears.

_____

_____

_____

_____

Are you afraid of speaking your truth when someone hurts your feelings or upsets you?

_____

_____

_____

_____

Are you afraid that you will not get promoted at work, or do you hold yourself back from climbing the ladder?

_____

_____

_____

Are you afraid that someone important to you is going to hurt or leave you?

_____

_____

_____

_____

Are you afraid that you will not have enough money to do all the things you want to do?

_____

_____

_____

_____

List all of your fears that come up when you ask yourself what you have been afraid of that is currently holding you back, or keeping you from moving forward.

_____

_____

_____

_____

Review your fears. Is each of these fears valid? If not, explain.

_____

_____

_____

_____

Maybe one of your fears is that someone you love is not going to love you back. Ask yourself if there were a wall around you and what would it look like? Is the wall tall or thick?

_____

_____

_____

_____

Is the wall close to you?

_____

Is the wall surrounding you completely?

_____

Maybe it's time to dissolve the wall, so that you can allow yourself to grow and accept others in your space.

List your happiest memories, people, activities, etc. that bring you joy and happiness.

_____

_____

_____

_____

Did your mother or father get you a favorite toy or take you on a vacation somewhere?

_____

_____

_____

_____

Did your best friend make you laugh so hard you cried?

_____

_____

_____

_____

Did you meet a stranger that touched your life?

_____

_____

_____

_____

Did you help someone recently that meant something really special to you?

_____

_____

_____

_____

List all of your joys that have brought you happiness or laughter.

_____

_____

_____

_____

What are some things that make you smile?

_____

_____

_____

_____

Do you have a pet that you play with and keeps you company?

_____

_____

_____

_____

When you see someone smiling at you, do you smile back?

_____

_____

_____

_____

When you watch something funny on T.V. or a romantic movie that warms your heart, what exactly is it that puts a smile on your face?

_____

_____

_____

What makes you laugh?

_____

_____

_____

_____

Is there a special friend or relative who makes you laugh
uncontrollably when you spend time together?

_____

_____

_____

_____

Do you laugh when you watch comedies or read books?

_____

_____

_____

_____

Where do you find laughter in your life?

_____

_____

_____

_____

As you begin to awaken and release your inner dialogue, you
may begin to write up your own questions by hand. When you start

to write consistently, you embark on who you are deep inside, and your writing becomes an excellent reflection and resource of information for you to better understand the essence of yourself and what is important to you. Being able to realize who and what makes you smile and laugh will remind you to keep in touch with those people and places.

When you find what is good for you and feels right, then remember those good feelings and thoughts and write them down. It's great to keep a journal of all of your positives, so that if you are ever feeling sad, afraid, or out of balance, you can go in and read your journal and feel all of the love that you have experienced. Once you start reading these positive memories, you will begin to feel the joy surrounding you and remember just how loved you always are.

"You have every single emotion and every single gift inside of you because we are all one. "You are all the children of the earth, and so you are all from my veins. And, because you all drink from my water and eat from my womb, you are all the same. I see that some of you feel that you must destroy yourself to build yourself back up. Right now, some of you do not feel worthy to be alive when you awake. My children, when you breathe in the sacred breath of life, you are worthy. You are each so very loved."

There may come a time when you realize there is no time, there is no "knowing," and you are in the moment, and it's now like living as if it were your last day to live. You now have nothing holding you back, and you know that it is your last week without any limitations; what would you do? Earlier I asked the question, "What do you want to do with your life?" Now I am asking you to imagine that you have no limitations of time or money or anyone judging you or holding you back. You are now free to do exactly what you want, spend as much money as you want, and go anywhere you want at any time. List all of the places and things that you would do with your life without limitations or restrictions of time.

Explore More Deeply

Here are some further questions to spark your creativity:

Who is important in your life that you want to see?

Do you have any relatives that live far away or ones that you have never met?

Do you have an old friend from elementary or high school that you remember fondly?

_____

_____

_____

_____

(Chances are, if you have thought about them over the years, they have thought about you, too!)

Maybe there is an actor, or someone who has changed your life, that you want to meet or write them a thank-you letter. If there is anyone alive that you want to see or meet for the first time, then who is that person(s)?

_____

_____

_____

_____

Change Your Life from a "One Day" person to a "Today" person!

What places does your heart and inner voice tell you to go that you have not yet listened?

_____

_____

_____

_____

Did you imagine yourself on a cruise ship ten years ago to the Caribbean, but never bought the ticket, or got your passport? Where do you want to go?

_____

_____

_____

_____

Do you feel drawn to travel to Europe, or to a historical or sacred site that you read about or saw in a movie that keeps crossing your mind?

_____

_____

_____

_____

Sometimes places that you feel drawn to go will have a significant meaning in your life and that's why you are drawn to go there. When I went to Guatemala in 2007, there was a great amount of physical suffering that was released there and many important people that are in my life now. After you have thought about the people you want to see and places that you want to go, evaluate what the fears and blocks are that are holding you back. Perhaps it's a perception of time and money that is holding you back. Here are some detailed questions you may want to ask yourself if you do have dreams of traveling and meeting people.

Is there the fear of leaving children behind with someone to watch over them, or taking them with you? Is there fear of spending too much money and then not having enough? Is fear present of not being worthy to go see someone that you love and miss? Are you afraid that someone you love is not going to remember you or want to see you? What are the fears that keep you from following your heart's path? Remember that most of our fears are illusions and that maybe less than 5% of them are real. The best way to find out your follow your path is to follow your heart and instincts on journeys that may change your life in ways that you never imagined.

If you would like, make a copy of your lists and place it somewhere where you can see it and update it from time to time. It's also good to make a vision board of all of the people and places that you want to see and visit. Another suggestion is to make a list of your "goals" by placing the answers to these questions directly on your list of places to visit and people to see. Be creative and have fun creating your desires as there is no limit to your imagination. Take the time to honor and respect yourself by believing that you deserve everything that you want to accomplish in this lifetime.

"Your respect and compassion for others are the respect and compassion that you have for yourself and for this world. We all live on this earth together, and no matter how far apart you live from each other, what you do will have an effect on everyone here. Just put your ear down to the earth and ask from your heart; I will tell you. Travel to the mountains and

listen to your relatives, the rock people (stone people); they are here to guide you. Ask the stone people what gifts you have if you do not know, and they will assist you on your path. More than likely it's something that you dream of doing or love to do but are yet to take the time to figure it out or too afraid to do it. Do not fear time and do not fear power, for both are very, very precious like each and every minute that we have here on earth.

"Do you not understand that the oceans can cleanse the entire earth in less than a day, that fires can cleanse the earth in less than a day, that winds can cleanse the earth in less than a day? The elements are sacred; the earth, the water, the fire, and the air. Do you take time to thank your water, your fire that heats your home, the air that you breathe in with every single breath you take, shallow or deep? Each one is sacred, and each one has the power to cleanse whatever you need it to, whether it's mental, physical, or spiritual. It is your heart that needs to be heard. Your words are powerful, but your heart is how we are all connected. Your heart that beats with mine each time, each and every living being on this planet, we all beat together as one. And as long as you allow yourselves to survive on this planet we will always beat as one. There is no one here alive that is more important or higher or above anyone else. There is no perfect one that is going to save you or guide you, as we are all guided as one. Each one of you has come to this earth to partake in cleansing and healing and to experience these wonderful emotions, such as sadness and happiness, heartache and love.

"There is not anything or anyone more powerful than another; you are equal, and sometimes that is very hard to believe as each person wants to feel special. Could you imagine having over six-billion children, or even one-hundred children? Now, imagine what that would be like to make each and every one of them feel special when they will not even look at you or acknowledge you. How can I tell you just how special you are to me when you won't even take five minutes to walk barefoot or to stop and listen (by placing your ear to the earth) to what I have to say? Sounds silly listening to the *earth, right? Sounds funny listening to your body, right? Sounds funny to listen to a tree, right? When is the last time you heard your body talk or a plant talk? If you do, what do they say? Is your body tired and lonely because you are running so fast you can't stop and listen? Are the plants and trees lonely in your surroundings? What about your water? Is it nurtured and cared for before you drink it? What are you sharing with your food and water, because it is always sharing with you? The water, plants, and trees (medicine) love you."*

For some of you, reading these messages may seem bizarre or silly to consider, for others this may seem like common sense. Sometimes, when something does not make sense in the moment, you will have an experience when it all comes together. If you are unfamiliar with speaking to your body, or to trees, then I can honestly say that it does not hurt to try this at home. Later on, I will focus more specifically on the trees as helpers and what you can do in your own time to connect with them. Humans have survived with the help of the tree nation for numerous years. I am surprised at the minimal knowledge that is shared with children about trees and adults in universities. All of Mother Nature and the elements are a vital part of our existence, yet many of us do not learn about this powerful knowledge until we are adults, if at all.

Mother Nature includes all of the mountains, terrains, volcanoes, trees, plant life, ocean life, and more. The elements-earth, water, fire, and air-are all important and vital to our everyday living, yet we have forgotten how important it is to learn about and honor them. The earth helps to ground us and provides abundance in the material realm. The earth also clears away any negative energy that is in our energy field and our chakras (energy centers inside the body).

Water helps to keep us flowing freely with all of the rapid changes that surround us at all times. Water is the element emotion, so it helps us to release our emotions that no longer serve us. Fire helps to cleanse, renew, revitalize, and bring forth energy that is constantly moving as everything is made of energy. Fire also helps to magnify your intentions and make them more solid. The air is what we breathe to connect with to one another in the material and spiritual world on earth. The air also helps to move us through changes and guide us where we need to go. Through doing deep breathing, you can release, cleanse, and balance all aspects of your life. All of these elements are also nations just as all of the people of this land were nations. Everything that has energy is alive and is therefore deserving of respect, compassion, and love.

Here is a great suggestion that was shared this year in California for ceremony: each time you take a bath and shower, it would be respectful to say thank you, especially if you are asking for cleansing at that time or consciously detoxing in hot baths or springs. The water is here to assist you and sustain you in various ways. Think about how much of your physical body is made out of water and all of the foods and drinks that we consume.

"The same percentage of water I have in my veins is the same proportion of water that you contain in your veins. Scientists have figured out every fact that people need to prove that we are all similar life forms and energies. For example, scientists know that trees are from the same DNA building blocks as humans, and plants and trees give us medicine, natural medicine, and that plants will grow around you when you are sick, the plants that you need to survive. The plant people will grow around your home or land to be there for you as food and medicine. The trees, plants, and roots are there for you whenever you need them. Sometimes, the trees and plants get poisoned and ripped out and burned, and they cry, but they do not hold grudges. They will all come back again and again as long as there is life here to help. The tree people and plant people are your medicine when you are sick or sad, when you are wounded or dying. The tree people and plant kingdom need respect and love just like any two-leggeds, four-leggeds or ones that swim, crawl, or fly.

"Each and every living being here on this planet needs to feel the love and respect from you. When you are able to respect yourself, then it will be simple to respect all of life. When I say, all of life, this includes all humans, as well as animals, trees, flowers, plants and all living things. It is time to take a look at your surroundings and see if you are respecting your close relatives, friends, and loved ones. All animals, insects, trees and life really need a lot of love and attention. If you are already respecting your elders by living with them and feeding them and keeping them company, then you might want to broaden your mind more and start respecting your elder trees. The elder trees are the stronger, wiser ones whom carry great medicine."

I once spoke with a man named Michael who worked with a 2,000 year old Yew tree in Scotland. He spent years with the tree, and utilized the medicine from the tree for his healing. He said that he went through many different changes and some sickness while he was healing. Many helpers and teachers all over the world have learned many different ways for natural healing from trees. It's like trusting a one-hundred-year -old elder healer as opposed to trusting a five-year-old healer. I cannot express enough about the thousands and millions of plants, vines, and trees that are all over the world for you, for everything you need. I believe that it is only the material world with wealth, houses, cars, and western medicine that have blinded the sight of all the love and medicine right before us, beneath us, above us, all around us, and right within ourselves.

Since there has been greed here for many moons, many people put up emotional and mental walls and barriers including one of the worst barricades, fear. These fears and hindrances have created limited vision in our teachers and leaders and even some of our elders. Currently, it's time to learn to see, hear, and speak through your heart and through your soul and surrender to the Creator and learn to accept the changes that are here now, this moment on earth. Working through your heart will help you to live in the moment and feel your connection to the earth, to the trees, and to each other. There are many resources around, so many of you must begin now. There is much preparation and effort to be completed. There is a great deal of assistance needed by our leaders, healers and teachers to facilitate with all of these little ones being born right now at this exact second.

Are You a Natural Born Leader?

Are You Ready to Be a Leader or Helper?

Here are some questions to ask yourself to see where you are on your path. And, for some of you

meant to be leaders, maybe there are some reminders here to help you stay on track.

Do you see yourself as a student, helper, or teacher?

_____

_____

_____

_____

How do you help your brothers and sisters?

_____

_____

_____

How do you help your elders?

_____

_____

_____

_____

How do you treat yourself as a human being?

_____

_____

_____

Is there anything that you want to change about the way you treat yourself?

_____

_____

_____

_____

How do you view the world we live in now?

_____

_____

_____

_____

Everyone has a story and everyone has a dream.

What is yours?

(This is a great question to journal when you have more time for yourself)

_____

_____

_____

_____

_____

_____

_____

_____

_____

_____

_____

_____

_____

_____

(You may want to take some time to write down your stories and dreams at separate times and share these with someone special when you are ready!)

After reviewing these questions, you may want to revisit what you wrote down at a later time, and see if your thoughts and actions have shifted. Pay attention to what changes that you want to make, if any at all, and then write down the transformations that you create. It is important to share your dreams with someone, and find someone to support you and assist you in reaching those goals and dreams. There are many people out there waiting to assist you.

My dream is to help as many people as possible have the fullest life while they are here on mother earth. My dream is for the children to be able to eat each day and not die in the heat or the cold because of lack of protection. I have seen the children and elders without water or electricity, but with black mold on the ceilings on the reservations throughout North America. When I tell people about the addictions in South Dakota, Oklahoma, or other reservations, they say that they had no idea children were drinking and doing drugs so young and committing so many suicides. Some people I meet started drinking around the ages of seven to nine years old. There are many people who have never even left the reservations that they were born on, and the thought of leaving terrifies them. Some people do not realize that reservations were prison camps. For most of the people that were moved to them were not able to leave without written permission by the people who placed them there.

I went to a Sundance ceremony once to look for a couple friends while I was traveling to South Dakota and Nebraska. While I was there, we were notified to pray for the family of a young four-teen year old girl that killed herself. Another recent suicide was one of my younger brothers, and I have to admit, it's the hardest way to lose someone that you love. When I was editing my book a couple of months ago, I had to move his name to my relatives on the other side, along with my mom's brother that passed away just a couple weeks later. I know that they are all watching over us and helping to guide us and keeping smiles on our faces the best way they know how. I remember to be thankful for the huge hug that I gave my uncle Ric in the Pawnee Community Garden. This was the last time I saw him in Pawnee and I cried so hard. Tears were flowing down my face before I even let him go, and when he and my mom drove away I sobbed. I was also blessed that I took a trip with my good buddy Jim to Montana October 2012 to see my dad and brother just months before he took the Journey home. I realize that not everyone knows when a relative is going to take the Journey, or be able to see someone beforehand, so I feel grateful for that.

It's time for us to stop and listen, to stop being so selfish and greedy, and to start sharing and helping our children. The children are the future of this planet, and how the earth is treated rests on them. The children depend on us to be a model of how to respect each other and the earth. Simply by living with respect in your home for each other, the water, land, plants and animals will teach your children to respect life. It is so important to concentrate on yourself first, because what surrounds you is the reflection of what is inside of you. The Creator already has a divine plan. It's now up to us to slow down and listen to our inner voice and messages that we receive from the universe. These beautiful children are the hope for mother earth to survive the next seven generations.

I want to live to see mother earth being respected once again; to see our elders being respected once again; to see the trees being loved once again as our relatives. My dream is to see the waters clear again and to drink from the free flowing streams of the earth that the rock and mineral people have cleansed for us from the great oceans and seas. My dream is for the ones that swim in the ocean to survive with us two-leggeds and with all of the little creepy crawlers and forest relatives to survive without their homes being destroyed anymore. I fear that if we do not start respecting ourselves, each other, and the earth, we may continue to keep losing populations as well as poisoning our waters and land.

From my heart, directly to yours, I love you. I hope that each and every single one of you may one day want to stop hurting yourselves and each other. I hope that the elements: the earth, the water, the fire, and the air will start to feel respected and cared for again, for the reason that enough of the two-leggeds are taking just a few minutes a day to give their gratitude. Offering respect and compassion for all that we have on this planet is to provide healing for the elements. For example, since we are connected to the earth and the water and all elements and things, what we say and do affects on the world around us. When you say something hurtful to someone, or about someone, you may cause them emotional or physical pain.

Afterwards, you may decide that you want to apologize to them, or make peace through forgiveness and love. Therefore, the words that you said to that person were toxic, and it made them mentally or physically ill. Sometimes, there are no words, and a person ignoring someone has caused them mental or physical suffering. Because stress from thoughts and the mind has an effect on the physical body, a person will more than likely suffer headaches and depression before the pain manifests in the physical body. When there are no words, or no action, then there is loneliness, which is suffering and neglect. This, too, is hurtful and may be seen as contaminate to the mind, and therefore, to the body.

The concept of what you say and do is the same for our planet, including the elements and the animal and plant kingdom. Everything and everyone needs to be loved and respected by a "hello," spending time together, with them, or through an offering of some sort. An offering could be a hug to the earth or a tree. An offering is a gift of any kind, as long as it comes from the heart. Some people show their love by offering silver coins under a tree, sharing some water around the roots or singing healing songs to the waters. Other people show their love by dancing on the earth, creating fires to clear the land and give her nourishment with the ashes. The most important offering is giving time of yourself and simply listening or just sitting on the earth or in the water. One of the best ways to connect to the earth and to yourself is to simply sit with your back against a tree and ask that tree to connect its universal flow of energy with you while you sit and relax. Then, when you are finished just say thank you and disconnect with the tree by offering a hug or clapping your hands. Whatever way you feel comfortable giving thanks will work. It is always the intention behind your actions that is recognized by our life source, mother earth.

CHAPTER TWO

₪ Reflections & Perceptions

"Be what you are. This is the first step toward becoming better than you are."

~Julius Charles Hare~

My Creator's name is Love. Love has no gender, and Love is everything. Love is the wind, the storms, the thunder, the lightening, the elements, the trees, the two-leggeds, four-leggeds, and all of life that exists on this planet. Love made all the different worlds, dimensions, and parallels so that we could all support each other. Love created the "natural" world with enough for us to sustain ourselves which includes: plants, trees, animals, and living organisms. Love is the circle or the spiral of life where everyone and everything as we know it is a part of everything. Here on earth, we attend school by learning from one another through words, actions, experiences and my favorite, sharing knowledge, wisdom, and compassion.

Reflections are what and who you see around you every day, and your perception is how *you* see the world and people around you. Your personal relationships include your family, friends, job, and surroundings in general. Your family is not always your blood family, and your friends are not always life-long friends. I have found my family in my travels and when I move to different states. Family is someone that is there for you when you need a friend, a place to live, a plate of food, and someone to laugh or cry with. Family is sometimes from a previous life that did not get reborn into the same blood-line, yet when they see your face, they remember you from long ago somewhere. The people that are in your life will be there for the moment in time needed to serve a purpose on your journey.

I remember a few years ago when I asked to view life from the standpoint of my higher self. I asked the Creator to present only the higher self in others and for all illusions to fall away. I had a trip planned with some friends out-of-town, and on my way there, one of them told me not to come. I was very confused, and I decided to continue on my journey and stay with some other friends. While I was in town, I ran into my friend that told me not to show up. She was with some other friends that I also knew, and they acted excited to see me.

I did not understand exactly what had happened, except for learning in trusting the universe that they were no longer needed in my life. One thing that I hear over and over from my elders and guides is to stop being so nice and giving to people who only take from me and to listen to my intuition and my gut feelings right away. I tend to think I am being nice by spending time around people who I know are only draining me; I think that I am helping them, but I am not. It is always important to trust your intuition and move on when something does not feel right. Ultimately, being in alignment for the highest good of all humanity is what I pray and hope for.

The only thing that I claim to know is that there will always be change, and that we live in circles, or spirals. Circles mean that we will go around and repeat again what has happened in the past. If you place close attention, you can watch your own inner-circles and if there is a pattern that you would like to change, then you can monitor your cycle and see what is working for you and what is not. Viewing your life in the spiral is working up and down through the earth's energy, up to the universal energy. The earth's energy is what grounds us in the present moment. The universal energy connects you to everything in and outside of the earth. It's melding the future with the past and showing us in this present moment that we call the now.

Spirals are like a roller coaster to me. You go up, up, up,

getting higher and higher on life, and then all of a sudden, you hit the top. While you are floating on cloud nine, everything seems so perfect, happy, and free; then, boom, gravity strikes! Just like that saying, "You burst my bubble," you will come right back down to earth. Something hits you, the downward spiral. But this instant, you remember some lessons from that last spiral ride you took. This time you decide to act with love and compassion from a compassionate place without selfishness. You decide you have learned this lesson and now it's time to move on to the next level. Otherwise, you may decide that you have learned this lesson, and you enjoy it, so you decide to stay in this same pattern, because it brings you and others joy.

The circle of life means that all things have already happened and life will continue on. In a circle, there are no permanent stops or cracks. Life is a continual process that has been created, and it is up to us to flow with the curves and changes that will always occur. Trusting that your path is already in place is having faith in following your heart and your spirit.

When you are not accomplishing or reaching your goals, you are experiencing a lack of faith in the universe and in yourself. We are only humans here on earth, and sometimes we are hard on ourselves and think that we are not supposed to make mistakes. It is only through learning from mistakes and the love and energy of the universe that we can continue to survive here. Make sure that the reflections of people and places are at least your truth and that you are not living in illusion or a feeling of being where you do not belong. It is never too late to make changes, because changes are never-ending, like the circle of life. Here are some wonderful questions to see where you are at on your path.

If you wish, take out your journal and write down any questions and answers that you feel drawn to answer.

Where do I currently see myself on the learning path and what all do I want to learn?

_____

_____

_____

_____

Do I perceive myself as enjoying life to the fullest?

_____

_____

_____

_____

What currently brings me joy?

_____

_____

_____

_____

In my circle of friends and family, does my world contain hope and happiness? Explain.

_____

_____

_____

_____

My perception of love includes the following actions, words, and gestures.

_____

_____

_____

_____

How do I give and receive love regularly?

_____

_____

_____

_____

Reflections encompass everything you observe around you but, more precisely, how you perceive them. The same surroundings that you and others are in will be perceived differently by each person there. Just today, I went to search for a coffee shop in west Wichita, and when I came across the first one I saw, I was certain the shop was brand new. It had been about three months since I had been in the same shopping area. But, when I asked how long it had been there, she told me three years! It's amazing how things can magically appear when you are more aware of your surroundings. With so many beautiful experiences to share in just one day here on earth, it overflows my heart with gratitude and amazement for this world we know as earth, and my mother.

We all live in this world together, yet this world is our own for each of us. We create our worlds by our own inner thoughts, choices, desires, and strengths. Human beings are one of the most powerful living organisms known in the universe. Although we have guides and ancestors looking over us, we still have will power. Look at a tree, for example. They are a living organism just as you are, yet they do not worry that they are going to grow twenty feet high and look beautiful in the summer and spring. They just begin sprouting and growing and flourish and create fresh air, food, and medicine for us to survive. I looked into the eyes of a baby the other day, and she looked back into mine. There was a divine embrace through our eyes and I felt no judgment, no worry-just peace and love. This is the feeling that we all hold deep within our souls that we may forget after we are confronted with the experiences of life on earth.

You are the full spectrum of life with free will. You can choose to flow with the divine, flow with your mind, or flow with whatever you choose from day to day. In your mind, utilizing your vast imagination, you can create and *do* create the world as you know it today. You are love, you are light, you are strength, and you are everything you give yourself the power to be. You have heard this before, time and time again, but for some reason it just hasn't set in the subconscious mind yet. How many times have you told yourself the following: "I have to do this. Why can't I do this? I have to quit this. I need to finish. Why is it taking so long? Why is this so hard for me? What? When? Where? Why?" All of these questions you ask yourself are all of the expectations that you may have for yourself. But, do you really know why? Why do you feel that you have to get something done in a certain amount of time? Do you have the weight of the world on your shoulders? Perhaps you don't feel motivated or you feel defeated and have no drive in life.

Either way, it may be time to find out why you see the way you see, why you think the way you think, and why you want what it is that you want in this lifetime. Possibly now is the time to be genuine and direct with yourself, to start living as your true self now. When you are living as your true self, you are also loving yourself and allowing yourself experiences, such as patients, compassion, and excitement! You become the person that chose to be alive to love, to learn, to forgive; and to experience joy, happiness, and self-love. Maybe it is your turn to get inspired and get motivated before your time runs out. Are you going to let your time run out here on earth? Or, are you going to utilize your time here to the best of your amazing, gifted, and powerful potential!? Yes! When you are ready, grab a notebook and a pen, and let's get started on finding that inner, amazing you! These will be a series of questions to get your creativity started with finding out who you are and why and if you are being your true authentic person.

For each of these questions, take the time to elaborate on your answers and see what comes up in your mind, heart, or intuition.

Where am I right now? Honestly, am I really happy here?

_____

_____

_____

_____

What am I wearing today and why?

_____

_____

_____

_____

Am I comfortable?

_____

_____

_____

_____

What colors do I typically wear?

_____

_____

_____

_____

Do I accept my physical body, mental body, spiritual body?

_____

_____

_____

_____

What do my clothes that I'm wearing represent to me?

_____

_____

_____

_____

Do I dress in comfortable clothes no matter where I go?

_____

_____

_____

_____

Do I work and attend events where I have to dress up?

_____

_____

_____

_____

Close Up and Personal.

Now take a look at your face.

Are you wearing makeup? What do you see?

_____

_____

_____

_____

Do you worry about your skin, such as acne or wrinkles?

_____

_____

_____

_____

Are your eyes healthy?

_____

_____

_____

_____

Are your teeth healthy?

_____

_____

_____

_____

Do you hide your real face to the world?

_____

_____

_____

_____

Are you shy or ashamed to look people in the eyes?

_____

_____

_____

_____

Do you enjoy eye contact with other people?

_____

_____

_____

_____

Do you tend to stay connected to the world and other people, or do you stay disconnected?

_____

_____

_____

_____

Do you take good care of your hygiene?

_____

_____

_____

_____

Is your hair clean, nicely placed, shaved, or trimmed?

_____

_____

_____

_____

Are you comfortable in your natural state, or do you wear a mask or two?

_____

_____

_____

_____

Did you have siblings?   If yes, do they have an influence on how you dress and look?

_____

_____

_____

_____

What qualities or traits do you see in yourself that you recognize from your parents, school friends, or other relatives?

_____

_____

_____

What reflections did you see that you took on in life?

_____

_____

_____

_____

As you read these questions, begin to let your memories flow, and jot down anything that comes to mind. You do not have to answer every question, and please write some of your own questions to yourself. This process might take a few hours or maybe a few months to a few years to go through. Learning who your actual self is will take some time and dedication. Especially after many years of not realizing that some of the things you do are mainly influenced by other people. Reflections of others and not your authentic self may include what you say, the places you go, the place you work, or even the personal relationship that you are in or not. After you discover some of the answers to these questions that you have not asked yourself before, you may change your perception of yourself.

As you look through different lenses in your own world, the reflections of those around you may begin to change rapidly. This may be difficult for some of you, as change for the better is often times more difficult than change for the worse. From previous experience in workshops, I know some will breeze through this self-learning process, and most will not even try. If you want, I suggest reading your questions and answers out loud and repeating this exercise from time to time to see the changes you have made. It also helps to communicate this with someone, especially if you are having tribulations with various questions. And, more than some people realize, a lot of us are suffering from the same experiences and stories that we can't let go of that keep replaying in our minds. Your thoughts may include how sad and lonely and unhappy you are, or how much you dislike your body. Maybe your thoughts are painful experiences from your parents, or past, and now you see reflections of this pain in your life. All of these thoughts can replay over in the mind, and you feel like there is nothing that you can do about it.

So now, the first thing to do is to rid any negative thought patterns and doubts that you have practiced for so many years. You know what these patterns are, because you keep seeing them occur in your life and you are tired of them. For some reason the same thoughts are a comfort to you every day saying, "Yes! I am here!" When you feel it's time to say goodbye and thank you, then it's time to move on. Your gut instincts will let you know when there is a negative pattern that does not belong in your life. First, forgive yourself for judging that you were afraid to change and being worried about everything all of the time instead of trusting.

Worries are like weeds in the garden. They are not bad; weeds all have very good medicine. They are a part of the plant kingdom and often dandelions are ripped out and tossed to the side even though they can be used in salads and are very medicinal for the stomach and various ailments. I say weeds are like worries because you cannot simply pull out a weed and expect it never to grow back. What if the earth is all hard and dried up and the weed is old and deep-seated? That means you need to soak the earth first, or in other words, you need to nurture that worry root, by soaking it, and then pull it out. Huge change does not happen overnight. If you are simply stripping the weeds out of the earth, then it may cause more pain and suffering than needed, and, on top of that, the weed will just come right back anyway because it was not removed with love. Simply start day by day, retraining these thought patterns with new positive affirmations instead of the previous negative ones. Start with drinking water each day when you wake up and giving the water thanks before you drink it. There are many things that you can do to be mindful of yourself and all of creation around you that sustains you.

Each morning, begin to ask yourself a few questions out loud in the mirror or writing down on paper to change your thought patterns. For example, ask yourself, "Self (state your name), why are you so afraid to lose weight and be attractive? Why are you so afraid to have a beautiful smile with great teeth? Why are you so afraid of the dark? One night I asked myself that very question; I actually yelled into the dark silence, "Why I am I afraid of the dark?!" The reply was nothing. There was silence and a sense of deep inner peace at that moment of nothingness, and that night I slept soundly. Ever since then (only about three years ago), I have slept peacefully in the dark. Since we are all related, the world is a reflection of all of us put together and the more you understand that, the more your energy and thought will bring positive changes to the earth for each other. When looking at the world as a mirror reflection, the more you balance the ego, the more other people around you will be balanced as well.

The clearer that you allow yourself to be, the clearer the world will become around you. It sounds very simple, but the truth is for some of you this may be hard, and for some of you it may be simple. I like to say out-loud in sacred space, "Creator, please allow me to desire all of the things that I need in my life to walk a balanced path for myself and all of creation." I heard someone say that what you desire is not good, and I thought to myself, I am glad that I pray to desire what I need and not make up specifics about what I think I need!

The more you seek inner balance, the more you will attain inner balance; therefore, the more balanced the world will become around you. "Seeking," "wanting," "accepting," and "replacing" are all great words to ponder while going through a transition period to find inner balance and peace. Once you choose not to allow mind and ego to control your life and the world around you, you will begin to live without them. You will soon notice, when the time is right, how others around you are living without the ego as well.

Ego is like the water. It is a vital part of the physical world and, therefore, vital for our bodies. It is important to respect the ego just like it is important to respect the water. Ego helps us with our strength and courage and vitality, but is detrimental when used for power, greed, and control. Remember that saying, "you will never know until you try?" Well, you will never do without trying either. In order to do, you must first try. Trying is like taking a baby step; it's like the little doer that finally did! One day you just tried, and come to find out, you didn't try; you did it! Try to live to your full potential, try to live without anger, jealousy, and sadness. It is up to you to create the happiness inside of you. Create the reflection that YOU want to see each and every day for yourself, and for future generations to come!

For those of you that would like an example, here are some example responses of how someone might answer these questions: I am a business lady; I own a law firm. I wear suits every day. I go to the coffee shop down the street to get a low-fat latte, read, or work on paperwork after I leave the office. I am always watching my weight, and although I think my body is impressive, I still wish I looked better when I see other women that I think look stunning. Wearing strapping clothes makes me feel strong and secure. My mental health needs some minor improvement. I have a glass of wine when I get home, and I get lonely sometimes, as I have been single all my life. I went to law school right after high school, and my mother expected me to grow my own firm as my father did before he passed away. I hardly ever dress in comfortable clothes. Matter of fact, I wear silk pajamas at home even though I sleep alone, and oftentimes I am uncomfortable in them. I wear makeup, and I apply my night cream and eye wrinkle cream every night to keep my skin looking young and smooth.

Continue to follow through with the questions being as honest and detailed as possible. The deeper you go and the more time you give yourself to work on this process, the more you will realize others' reflections in you. Then proceed to the next step of who is this reflection. Is this you, your mom, your dad, your friends, or other relatives that you see as your mirror? Once you have finished with this reflection process of yourself, then you can go a step further and look at the reflection of yourself in your home, your workplace, and your personal relationships. Are you ready? Great!

Now, let's take a look at your living conditions. Do you own your own home or rent? Take a minute to write down where you live if you own or rent and why and how you feel about your living situation. Reflect on that choice and write about it. I suggest that you journal on this subject at least once a day for a week and see where it takes you. It's good to know why you are doing the things you do so that you can see the source of this action. If you are not happy or satisfied with anything in your life, then you are now able to look at it and realize that it's time to make a change for the better. If you feel that your living situation is something you need to work on, write more details. Otherwise, just jot down rent or own, home or apartment, love it or want to leave it.

Next, let's take a look at the inside of your home. Is your home clean, cluttered, or messy? Do you have useless junk that needs to be cleaned out of the closets or storage? Do you have expired food in the cabinets? Maybe it's time to give some cans and boxes to a children's or homeless shelter. What's going on in there? This can be a lengthy process, and for some you may need to call in some support. Your home is a reflection of your mind and, therefore, your body and spirit as well. The space in which you reside is your sacred space, your sanctuary. If your home is cluttered, you may have too many irons in the fire at once. If you have too many cobwebs and dust, you may have a lot of old memories and mind blocks that you need to clear out. If you have a lot of clutter and boxes, then you may have low energy, or perhaps heart problems are blocking the energy flow. You may also have sewage or plumbing problems if you have resentments and feelings of being unsafe in this world. Your home should be a place where you feel safe, loved, relaxed, and where you can unwind. At home, you want to be free to be yourself without judgment or any expectations from yourself or others. However, you also want to make sure that you are not living in clutter and holding on to unused objects.

Next, let's take a closer look at your material belongings.

How are your closets arranged?

_____

_____

_____

_____

Do you keep lots of shoes that you never wear or old clothes you cannot fit?

_____

_____

_____

_____

Do you have a lot of different interests that keep you changing gears and clothes and styles, or do you have a shopping addiction?

_____

_____

_____

_____

Is it time to clear out some useless junk or even some brand new items and give them away?

_____

_____

_____

_____

How is your bedroom looking?

_____

_____

_____

_____

Is there clutter under the bed or in the drawers?

_____

_____

_____

_____

Is it time to finish going through all that paperwork and useless junk?

_____

_____

_____

_____

Do you hold on to every little thing that you might use maybe once every three years or even ten years?

_____

_____

_____

_____

What is there that you don't need, and what is the reasoning behind holding onto it? Is there sentimental value to some things that you never use?

_____

_____

_____

_____

Just Let It Go!

Do you have things that remind you of something painful or make you sad or angry? (This is something that should be done right away. If you have kept something that only causes you memories of pain or frustration, then it's time to allow yourself to let it go).

_____

_____

_____

_____

As you go through each room and drawer in your house, take a bag and a box and begin to get rid of all the things that no longer serve your highest good. When you begin, simply state out loud, "I am now letting go of all of the material things that no longer serve my highest good." You may also say, "I am now releasing the items that are not serving the person that I am today for the highest good for myself and all others." "I now release any and all attachments to the material realm, and I forgive myself for holding on to things that do not serve my highest good." When you have completed this exercise, you can now choose to state the following affirmation: "I am now in perfect alignment with all things around me for the highest good of myself and all others." "I am surrounded by love, balance, peace, and understanding." If you currently do not feel safe in your own home, then state the following affirmation each day, "I am now safe and loved." "I am guided, guarded and protected at all times." All that which surrounds you is how you nourish yourself. So, now is a good time to reach out and ask for help if you need it. Also, remember all of the children and people in need in your own community that you can give your unwanted "treasures." Each day is a brand new day, and only you can make the changes in your own life.

CHAPTER THREE

₪ Releasing Attachments

"I follow my inner compass and discard any beliefs that are no longer serving me. I go to the source. I seek truth."

~Tony Burroughs~

For what felt like the first time in my life, I desired to do nothing else in the world but be in that very moment. The passion and life that I felt vibrating through my lips awakened my inner heart and soul. Before we kissed that evening I had been crying and pouring out my heart to this person who I had met about one of the hardest days of my life.

Just the day before, I dropped out of college in the middle of biology class when I found out one of my dearest uncles passed away. That same day, I also ended a five-year relationship with the person I had known since a teenager and thought that we would marry one day. Because we had moved into a house together, I also had to move out of my house that same day. I had just gotten my own one bedroom apartment across town and was in college when I got the call about my uncle. So, after I finished help to pack up some things at my uncle's house, I had to go to my home with my ex and finish moving all of my furniture to my new one bedroom apartment across town. This day, was actually the last day I went to school at that University. Losing so many things in my life in one day sent me into an anxiety attack on the way to my deceased uncle's house. When I arrived, heart pounding out of my chest, I laid on my back and it felt like it was going to explode.

It seemed as if I was completely alone in a world where harmony and happiness appeared to be nonexistent my whole life. I was searching for an answer that I didn't even know the question to. So many doors were just closed in my face along with the loss of my uncle who I rarely ever got to spend time with. I just prayed all day for hope to be able to recognize the answer when given.

This passionate kiss ignited my spirit to rise up and dance and feel real hope for the first time. It felt as if our souls knew each other and I was going to be okay. I had spent my whole life in and out of bad relationships at home, or in personal relationships. Peace and happiness were not very common memories, and happiness and joy were not two words to explain my heart's condition. I do believe that lust and relationships may come and go, but real love will remain with passion and always in my heart. I do not need another person to bring this light; it already exists within my being, and I choose never to let it burn out ever again. After years of talking and spending time with this person, I finally realized that I had to let go of the attachment of the person. I thought for years that this was my soul mate because of the peacefulness that I had felt. After several years of continuing communication I finally released the attachment and gained an everlasting knowledge of self love.

Releasing attachments may very well be the hardest thing on earth. Since the strongest and most powerful force is love, and when you truly love something, it is so hard to let it go. My father told me in a letter once that if I ever find true love, to hold it tight and never let go. For many weeks, months, and then over years, I thought about this one person, this one passion that released so much energy and movement from my soul that I could not stand to let it go. It took years of pain and sadness; driving home in heart-wrenching tears from a short visit; sleepless nights after talking on the phone. Until finally one year I had the strength to release the attachment; the courage to release the pain. It was not that I released the love or passion within; it was that I had to free the attachment to the specific person, place, or time. With true love, there is no distance or time that will ever change anything. There are no attachments to a particular person, or any expectations. There is only love.

Just a few weeks ago, I was traveling with two very close friends in Tulsa, OK, visiting their close friends. One of their friends happened to not be feeling well. I am not sure what all my friends had told him about my background or work, but he knew that I was from the Pawnee Nation and did natural healing work. He asked me if I could look at his health for him and tell him what was wrong. After I scanned his body and wrote down a lot of notes for him, I asked if he believed in past lives. He said he did not, and so I asked if I could explain something that I could see was from a past life. Because I had told him about the bump on his head (without ever touching it or any way of knowing about it), some other physical illness, and other things that he knew was going on, he felt comfortable enough with me and told me, "yes."

What I saw was in a past life there was a very harsh separation of him/her and a lover. He had a broken heart; it literally had to wait for it to be healed when he reincarnated into this lifetime. After I told him this, he explained how he was born with a hole literally in his heart and how "GOD" healed it when he was eighteen years old. After I told him this story, (that his love from his past life had reunited with him again in this lifetime) he replied, "Yes, my heart was healed, thirty-three years ago when I met my wife." He and his wife are still together, and I was honored to have met him and be so welcomed in his beautiful home through mutual friends.

I hear people saying that you can't really die of a broken heart, but I do not agree. I think that people die of broken hearts all the time. When a significant other dies, and the person left is broken-hearted and feels life is not worth living, following in death is understandable. I hear of people that die shortly after their best four-legged friend dies because that was their only love connection left on earth. Not only is love a powerful force, but like with everything else, there is also an opposite, hate.

Sometimes, we end up hating the one's we once loved, and sometimes we end up loving the one's we hate. No matter which way you feel around the circle, one or the other will always exist, but it is your choice which one to act upon. Love will include emotions such as forgiveness, understanding, compassion and kindness. Hate will include emotions such as anger, hated, depression, selfishness, guilt and shame. The only person that we can make suffer from feelings and actions of hate is ourselves.

There is a distinct difference between the love of embracing time with a person or place and having an attachment with them. From the day we are born, we start forming fondness with our parents, family, relatives, and friends. Even when we are in the womb, we are forming familiarities with voices, sounds, vibrations, and energies of those around us, just as we are form our tastes buds, our likes, and dislikes by what our mothers eat and ingest. We also imprint our mother's emotions and vibrations, and yet deeper, their anger and love. An attachment means that there can be negative results and painful feelings, or what people call drama. I learned the hard way that some people need to have an attachment to someone else at all times because they are not happy with themselves. There are different ways that people explain attachments and reasons for them. Some people will call people addicts, or co-dependents. Whatever label you place on attachments, they are typically viewed as un- healthy, imbalanced, or emotional syndrome.

People talk about how kissing someone on the lips can take about three years to fade away, and sexual intercourse takes about seven years. There are different healers, cultures, scientists, and others who agree on a certain time limit that these intimacies affect the physical and spiritual body. Over thousands of years, there have been facts and research done on how the emotional, spiritual body has an effect on the physical body so far as sickness and mental health go. There are many years of research and evidence that prove that the spiritual body and etheric field play a huge role in our mental and our physical "illnesses." The history of the human mind and spiritual body can be dated back hundreds of years, thousands of years, or even millions' of years, depending on the person that is researching or writing about it. There are so many different studies from recent times revealing what archeologists have "dug" up and what people have interpreted, oftentimes making up their own "theories".

The simple fact is, is that we all encompass our own perception of what this world is about and what the world has been in the past and what its "supposed" to be like. The truth is that no one knows what it's supposed to be like. You have the saints and the gurus who believe that we are already perfect, yet they are out there teaching people that they are already perfect. Some people believe that it depends on your vibration levels; while others trust that somebody can judge that you are enlightened. Some people think the less you speak may mean the more you know. To some people, being quiet may mean that they are preparing for battle. We all acknowledge actions in a different way from what we have learned and who we are.

Attachments may also be to food, sex, alcohol, tobacco, or drugs. I say if you can go twenty-one days without something letting it bother you, then you are alright. I first heard about the twenty-one days in Reiki class about letting the mind change its pattern. I have also heard a lot of doctors and psychiatrists who work with people on addictions say that after three weeks of treatment, the mind will be reprogrammed. In some of the workshops I have attended on spirituality and finding your own power, we begin with all of the negative attachments that we are currently stuck in and then work on releasing them.

Over the past three years, I have remembered memories as a child that was lost, and I cried and released them in a workshop group setting. A lot of this work that I wanted to do on myself is what I enjoy sharing with others in classes and workshops. I understand how hard it is to release an attachment, but it's only enjoyable when the process is complete. It is absolutely amazing to me how one single person can carry so many attachments! I have been releasing attachments for many years and I still have more to go. I realize that each person is already enlightened, and we are here to learn and experience things continuously. Enlightenment is merely remembering and trusting that we are all from the same source: the universe, the great mystery, the Creator of all.

We are all one here, and no one is higher or lower; no one is right or wrong. We have to have the ying and the yang and accept what the creator has created in us. How do you know what that is? Simply put, I believe it's what makes you happy. I've heard from people who share about releasing attachments and have expectations similar to mine.

Having expectations is similar to having attachments because you are relying on a person, place, or thing to bring about a certain result. In doing so, you are blocking the flow of life, the flow of creation to happen through you and around you. When you think that a certain person will bring you happiness or joy, is the same as having an attachment because you are expecting them to bring you happiness and joy. I have learned through experience that you are the only person who can bring yourself happiness and joy and for that matter, you are the only person who can bring you love. Therefore, you can only love another when you love yourself and you can only offer someone else happiness if you make yourself happy.

I agree with millions of helpers that it's a great thing to spend time alone each day if you are in a relationship or live with relatives or friends. If you are single or in between relationships, then always view it as a blessing to be able to take the time to get to know your true self, as we are conditioned to mirror or copy others. It happens right in school, from books. We are taught just to believe what we read, as in history class without questioning. We are taught to trust certain people and others that we can't trust. Typically, we are taught to trust and love our families no matter what, even though many children and people are abused, mentally, physically, or sexually by their own mothers, fathers, brothers, and sisters.

We are not all brought up the same, as generations change year to year and century to century. Most people are not taught that our souls have been here before and that we bring things into our lives from the past lives. We hold onto things in this life that we have not forgiven in the past or debts that we did not pay or any anger, pain, or hatred that we did not heal from in our past live(s).

The truth is, everything is already in Divine order, and the Creator has control over everything, not anyone else. There is no need to be attached to the material world, but respect for all that you are given is necessary. All we need to do is to take care of ourselves and our loved ones and release the worry that we are not being taken care of. Release the ego that says we have to take care of the entire world and allow the Divine to flow though us, and not through our egos.

So what exactly is it that I need to clear out of my mind, body, and heart? Attachments are things like worry, fear, and doubt. For example, I worry that I will not get this job that I want. I worry that my husband is going to cheat on me. I doubt that I am going to make any new friends. I don't think I am good enough to like or especially love. I am not pretty enough because I need to lose weight. I do not think that I am smart enough to go to school. The truth is, all of the knowledge, love, and beauty are inside of us already, and we need to let go of the worry, fear, and doubt so that we can shine our love, lights, and divine spirits! If you re-read some of these, they are ironic. Thinking you are not smart enough to go to school, when that is where you go to get the smarts in the first place. These unknown worries and fears are what I see as illusions. You have to get past all the fears to see the truth. When we are one with ourselves, we are one with the Creator, with God, with love, with each other. There is beauty in every living thing, and it is OUR choice to see that, to experience that. It is our choice to live our dreams in our wakeful state, and not just in our minds or in our dream states.

One of my teachers taught me that if you dream about something in the dream world, then you can apply it here. Sure, I dreamed about bungee jumping off the Eifel tower in Paris. However, when I researched it the next day, I found that jumping off the tower with a parachute had been banned. There are some things in life that may be too late to do now, but how will you ever know if you don't dream, or even apply your dreams! So many people are just now learning to listen to their dreams. Did you know that you can listen to your children and communicate with your animals in your dreams? The dream world is a very good place to work though a lot of your personal fears and work with children that are encountering fears. The dream world is a very important place that many of us have forgotten about over the last few thousand years. You can work through any blocks of fear, jealousy, and attachments though this state.

Once you are ready to release attachments, the first thing to realize is that this is a choice you have. Releasing attachments does not mean this person or place will not be in your life, but that you are now allowing for the highest good for yourself and all others. If are having lots of angry people around you or angry feelings towards yourself and others, then you want to release attachments to anger. If you are having worries about money for material gain or food, then you want to release your attachment to money, fear, and the material world. Where there is an attachment, there is generally worry and fear, and those two emotions block the love and flow that you deserve. Everyone deserves what they need in life to sustain them, and it is available for all.

Now is the time to release attachments, beginning with the self-inflicted attached feelings that we have about ourselves. Personally, I have always had an attachment with viewing my physical self as unattractive, and since this view has been there since a small child, I have many attachments involved with this view. When you are releasing a negative thought or action pattern, or what some people term as addictions, there is usually more than just the recent reasoning or meaning behind it. Also, we may have an attachment to a person or an object because it reminds us of someone or something in the past. In order to release an attachment fully, you have to release the root, not just the dried leaves on the top!

There are several ways to release attachments. The most important thing is your intention and willingness to let go. Intention is one of the most powerful feelings or thoughts besides your heart center. You may act by your heart for the most part, but the mind is also a very powerful tool. It is always good to trust the Creator who knows what is for your highest good, and then allow that to unfold naturally. Speaking words out loud of what and who you want to release is the most powerful way. You can also choose to release any and all attachments that are no longer serving your highest good or your truth path. Make sure that if you choose to release your attachments that you thank them for what they taught you and for any experiences, and always release them with light and with love. This makes sure that it is safe, gentle, and effective for both people. If you release with anger or revenge, then you are only causing yourself more suffering.

One of the ways that I released attachments with people from my past was to start a sacred fire outside (maybe a candle or actual fire) and call on the four directions, all of the directions in between, the sky and stars above, and the mother earth below. Then I call on all of my ancestors, guides, helpers, protectors, and all of those for the highest good. After I created my sacred space and set my intentions, I began to call on my "attachments." The first time that I did this about ten people popped up in my head right away.

One by one, I would say I now lovingly release any and all attachments that I have with you. I thank you for our experience together, I love you, I appreciate you, and I release you with love and gratitude. Thank you; thank you; thank you. When you release an attachment, you want to make sure that you are sending the energy with positive vibrations and that you also fill yourself with that same love and vibrations. Remember, what you give out to the universe and to others is what you are giving to yourself. After the next few times I did this exercise outside, someone came up from years ago. I had no idea that I still had an attachment to this person, and I felt a lot of anger and sadness when this person came to mind. I made sure to talk to the "anger" that I felt and to give extra love and care to releasing and sending lots of love to this person and to myself and the universe.

Make sure when you are releasing any sort of attachment and you feel anger or pain, that you are aware of where you are "sending" that energy. I always suggest sending it to the universe, or to mother earth. The universe knows what to do with the energy, and so does the earth. They utilize that energy and appreciate us releasing it back.

Please remember to be gentle and patient with yourself on releasing attachments. The first step is to realize to what you are attached; the next step is to ask yourself why you have an attachment, and then, finally, you can slowly begin to release when you are ready. I have found out during the releasing sessions with myself that sometimes there are people that are still attached to me, and then I am able to release them. I simply ask for any attachments that are no longer serving my highest good to present themselves, and then I lovingly release them with songs and prayers. There is not a particular way to release attachments; so do what feels best for you. There is no right or wrong way to release attachments, however, I advise to state, clearly your intention out loud. In all aspects of healing, clearing, and talking to spirits and guides, this process has worked for me, ever since I was a child.

Do not rush this process of releasing and letting go, or you may feel overwhelmed. Simply begin and continue day by day this incredible progress that many have not attempted. As human beings, we tend to be afraid of change, and we also understand how the small things have bigger impacts on us as well. So, remember that a short five minutes of taking time to release any or all attachments could have an incredible impact on your life. Also, remember to be proud of yourself for each step that you take. Reward yourself with flowers, a massage, or something nice. Believe that you deserve all things that make you happy in this lifetime. After all, you will have a space cleared out in your energy field that needs to be nourished with love and gratitude. Baby steps are safe and beautiful and great for welcoming grace, compassion, peace, and understanding in this amazing and beautiful process.

There is not a need to rush this process, but to begin and continue day by day is an incredible progress that many have not attempted. As human beings, we tend to be afraid of change and we also forget how the small things have huge impacts on us as well. Therefore, remember that a short five minutes of taking time to release some attachments may result in wonderful and amazing changes in your life. Also, remember to be proud of yourself for each step that you take and reward yourself with flowers, a massage or something nice. After all, you will have a space cleared out in your energy field that needs to be nourished with love and gratitude. Baby steps are safe and beautiful and great for welcoming grace, compassion, peace and understanding in this amazing and beautiful process.

CHAPTER FOUR

₪ Accepting Change & Forgiveness

"To forgive is to set a prisoner free and discover the prisoner was you."

~Unknown~

Do you have parents that when you think of one, or both of them, it can bring instant tears or anger to your eyes? Do you have siblings that drive you crazy? Or, do you feel like they terrorized you or made you uncomfortable with the person that you are today? When I started to look back at my life, I realized that I was placing a lot of blame on my relatives still for the things that happened to me when I was a child.

Also, when I attended group meetings and seminars, I realized that everyone there was placing blame and hurt on one of their relatives. Some hurt was caused for parents not being there at all, getting a divorce, or being an orphan. Some children were physical, mentally, and sexually abused by their mother or father and brothers. There were lots of pains that were written, spoken and shared between us during a two day workshop.

I realized the more that I began to meet and talk to other people, the more we all had in common. We were all humans, and as humans, we all suffer painful experiences to grow. These painful experiences leave deep wounds that can cut like a knife, even when letting them go. What we have to realize, is that the sadness and anger of the past is what clogs up our emotional bodies and keeps us tied to the past. This must be forgiven by realizing that everything is a chance for growth and every day is a miracle. It also helps to realize that everything we experience has a more powerful purpose that we can only see once we accept these facts.

When was the last time you created a tree with your hands? How about the last time you created a human being with your hands? What about the teeny tiny seed that you planted to grow the tree. Do you think that you really created the water that you use to water the seed to make it grow? Did you create the ground that you planted the seed in?

All of creation was created for us already. This earth, the trees, the plants, the animals, all of life were placed here for us to work with, to live with, and breath with- to clothe us and to protect us and nourish us. All we have to do is respect all that we are given and begin to see the beauty and the life and love in what the Creator has provided. Some people sit around crying and praying every day, waiting for something extraordinary to happen, when there are extraordinary events and miracles right in front of them. The fact is that you are an extraordinary miracle; you are a part of this sacred creation. You are not separate; you are each a part of this earth and all that is included in this circle of life.

The point is there are "miracles"; everything *is* a miracle. Every day is a very sacred ceremony, in a very sacred place with lots of sacred tools. What I have learned from my elders is that when you are in ceremony, in this life, you live with respect and love for everything and all those around you. Also, when you love yourself, you love each other, and you will see *miracles* happen every day. Why, you ask, are there miracles happening every day? Because miracles *are* the world that we live in when we trust the Creator and the on-going process of creation.

Our minds and our hearts are now getting ready to clear themselves for peace. Some of us may feel that we already have an open heart and we are just mentally clearing out any blocks and judgments against the self or each other. Then, there are some of us who feel that our minds are completely ready and want our hearts to be open, but no matter what we do, our hearts don't seem to open up. And now, our mother earth is clearing and cleansing herself for peace. Time is running out in this turn of the spiral, and it is now time to make peace with yourself and with each other. When we are at peace with ourselves, we stop judging what the mind is thinking, and start observing more, once we have learned acceptance. Then, when we have peace within our heart, we will feel the connection to the mother earth again and, therefore, to one another.

The first step to finding peace in the mind and in the heart is to find out if there are things in your life that you do not accept about yourself, or about the world as you see it today. What is important for you in your lifetime that is hard for you to accept, and is there acceptance and forgiveness needed? What are the first thoughts that come to mind? Perhaps it is a relative or a situation that you do not agree with. Maybe there's a complicated circumstance in your personal life, at work, or perhaps you are frustrated over the economy.

For thousands of years, there have been wars all over the earth. When you desire to make a change to find peace, the only war that you will find is within yourself. Some people contain wars in their hearts, and some people have wars inside their psyche. Perhaps you have determined that you would like to live alone for the rest of your life because you believe that you will be happier that way. You may literally believe that you need to fight in a war, and, therefore, you are constantly in a battle at home, at work, and driving in your car. Whichever war you may find yourself in, there is a need to forgive and let go.

Forgiveness is not an easy matter, and I don't pretend for one minute to treat it as such. Many families and countries have fallen over non-forgiveness. People have sought war over the murder of their fathers and brothers and entire families and even entire tribes and races. Every race of people have been under war and experienced deep suffering a pain. This is not a painless experience to forgive and forget. I understand that you hear people say, including I, that things are simple and to accept change can take place instantaneously, but the truth is, loosing hundreds and thousands and sometimes millions of people in a very short time can be very devastating. There are many ways to explain what has happened in the past and what is being carried on in the present, but I want to concentrate on the healing of the past and not what the past has presented. Holding onto the past and all those stories, the way we fought to be separated, to be in control, to be the most powerful will only continue to cause more suffering and more death. It's time to forgive; with yourself, your parents, and your lineage.

We each have our own views and come from different backgrounds and upbringing, but as you can see here on Turtle Island, here on this land people call America, we are learning to come together as one again, as we existed many, many years ago. There is a place within us known as intuition, known as our feelings, known as our hearts where we are all connected. Our hearts do not have different colors and shapes; they do not have different names and different emotions. We all share the same heart beat, the same shape; and we are all connected through the same space on earth.

This is the period as we complete this cycle of our generation to give the children the opportunity to be united once again with peace, love, and freedom to be themselves and to live amongst each other on this land. It is time for us to put aside our anger and our pain for what has happened here on Mother Earth for so many years. It is time to let go of our outlived thoughts of greed and understand that we can live in peace once again here on earth if we can forgive what has happened in this lifetime and lifetimes before. It is not an easy task, but as hundreds and thousands become aware and learn to forgive, the peace and the oneness will fall into place.

Our children have continued to suffer for thousands of years because our hearts and souls have been connected to this old pain and anger of the distant past. The true compassion of the Creator can be felt and experienced as we choose to forgive, love, accept ourselves, and one another. We have a much greater chance of regaining peace and surviving here on earth by doing so. I believe that our Mother Earth and the Creator will see and feel our progress and create cleaner water, air, and all the things we need to survive for our future children and generations to come. Our part is to only take care of ourselves, as the earth and the universe already know how to care for themselves. What you see in the world around you is a reflection of what we all have created inside of our hearts, bodies, and minds.

Think for a moment about the connection that you have to your pet or child. Have you ever heard that a child or a cat and dog can sense when someone is "bad?" I have had friends bring their children to meet me for the first time and admit they were "testing" me. Very small children can sense a person's energy field that contains their intentions. There is a frequency, or a vibration that we all contain, and animals, humans, plants and every living organism reacts to one another through this vibration. Have you ever stood next to someone and wanted to hold your breath, or move away from them. Our bodies will actually shift closer or further away to something that is good or harmful to our vibration. Our connections to each other are a lot more than what's on the surface, in this physical form. This is where we have been conditioned to be stuck in the material, superficial, world where sex sells, and drugs and alcohol are the leaders of the future of our children. It's time to make a difference, and all you have to do is change yourself, for that is all we can do. Some of you may not me leaders that will go speak in front of a public audience, or the world, but you will be the guide and support of your family.

The elements, the trees, plants, and the seasons are all here to support our growth, and as we start to respect ourselves and one another, they will naturally cleanse and become clear and plentiful for us once again. It's time to trust that it's all right to forgive and to accept change as so many people find it very difficult to let go of the past and to accept change.

There is a purpose for each different season. Similar to the stages in our life, the earth undergoes stages in her life. There are certain foods that will only grow through particular times of the year. We are the same way, whereas certain times in our life, is when we will grow. For example, our brains and physical bodies grow until we reach our early twenties. There will be times for mental growth when you attend school, spiritual growth when you connect to the divine and earth, and emotional growth when you have a family and relationships.

No matter what season you are currently living in, it is up to you to put in your work and time for yourself and for the future generations. Maybe the truth is that you do not know what angers you or where your anxiety and frustration comes from, and now it's time to search and learn if that's what you need to do to forgive. For some, it may be hard simply to forgive and let go if you are not consciously aware of what your grudges are. It may be time to do some research and ask yourself and your parents. Also, if needed, we have the technology to get your blood tested to see where your lineage stems from. You may even have bloodlines from several different countries that you are not even aware of.

As some of you may acknowledge our souls reincarnate from past lives, and some of you believe that we only take on the karma. Often times we carry the pain and the emotions of what we have suffered in a past life and we still need to forgive the trauma that we suffered or that our families suffered. Reincarnation is the belief of the Egyptians from thousands of years ago, the Mayans, the Eskimos, the Native Americans, and many other nations. Through doing lots of spiritual work on families, I have also learned that some Catholics believe in reincarnation.

There are many different places and people that are here to help you on your journey, but you must want to forgive and change. Most importantly, you must do the work, and you will only do the work when you are ready. I would like to share some examples of words of forgiveness that I hope you find helpful, and I strongly suggests that you write all of the things that you feel you need to forgive and repeat them out loud every day. Even if I have named all of yours, you might want to make yours a little more personable by adding names or places to your sentences.

Forgiveness Affirmations

I forgive myself for being a procrastinator.

I forgive myself for not trusting my first instincts.

I forgive myself for not being motivated.

I forgive myself for not speaking my truth.

I forgive myself for blaming my mother.

I forgive myself for blaming my father.

I forgive myself for being impatient.

I forgive myself for not following through.

I forgive myself for being disrespectful.

I forgive myself for being hurtful in any way towards myself or others.

I now forgive myself fully and completely;

I now forgive myself fully and completely;

I now forgive myself fully and completely.

Here are some positive affirmations that you can say each day to help you with change.

Remember, release from the heart, then the mind and body and spirit will follow.

I now love and accept myself and live my life to my fullest truth and potential.

I am powerful, loving, strong, and talented and I love to share with the world, for the world is me.

I love to share with myself because I love and respect myself.

I am wonderful and beautiful and I am thankful for all of life's experiences.

I allow others to have their own experiences in this life.

I flow with the rivers and winds of life.

I appreciate and accept all of the people who are in my life today.

I love and accept myself just the way I am.

I am a radiant, wonderful, and kind person!

Add some of your own affirmations...

CHAPTER FIVE

₪ Be Yourself

"Be who you are and say what you feel, because those who mind don't matter, and those who matter don't mind."

~Dr. Seuss~

To be yourself, you must love yourself. Otherwise, you will always be trying to cover something up, or pretend to be something you are not. Therefore, you will always set yourself up for disappointment or unhappiness. This is the first understanding to finding your true self. You are perfect right now where you are in life. If you have this view of imperfection about yourself, then you are only judging yourself. There is no one else on earth that can judge you, but you. When I teach my students to work on other people, I express the importance of transference. Which means that how you feel may or may not be felt by the person you touch. The confidence and love that you have for yourself will also be how the people around you will feel about you.

When there is judgment, then you are not allowing yourself to love and nurture yourself, and therefore, it becomes difficult to love others and allow others to share their love with you. You will tend to let others use you, belittle you, abuse you, and cross boundaries if you do not fully love yourself right now.

Once you know that the plant you are rubbing on your arm to sooth you is causing a rash, you should stop rubbing it on your skin. This is the same for two-leggeds, if they rub you the wrong way, then maybe you should not allow them to rub on you at all. It may just be that you are pretending to be something you are not, and so you will attract others who are pretending just as well. It's not that they have to be the same way that you are, it's just the same energy of pretending whatsoever they can draw them near. Just be yourself, and you will start to attract other people with similar interests and likes, and life will become way more enjoyable!

I understand that sometimes to be yourself is easier said than done. It seems as though modern life does not allow you to be yourself. For example, some schools may have a dress code. Also, jobs and even night clubs have dress codes. You also have to know how to stand up for yourself and respect yourself. If you are out at a club or with some friends and someone touches you and it makes you feel uncomfortable, then let that person know how it makes you feel. When you tell that person that their hand on your back is making you uncomfortable, not only are you honoring your own feelings, but you are also allowing them to understand boundaries that they may have not understood. It is important to listen to your own feelings and honor them. When you are honoring your own feelings, you are honoring the feelings of other people around you as well.

Since we are all here together, we are all working and living together, helping each other by being mirrors and reflections of each other. We rely on one another to see ourselves, by judging what we say and what we do, by how others perceive us. For myself, I spent many years wondering and asking how other people perceive me. I will ask, "So, how do you perceive me?" "What were your first impressions of me when you first met me?" These first impressions helped me to gain an insight on how I was presenting myself to the world.

It is also different in many parts of the world with diverse cultures and distinctive gestures of showing and giving respect. It's illegal not to wear shoes, so people that have never worn shoes who want to come to the modern world would have to learn to walk in them! Imagine going to another country where they did not wear clothes or shoes and you would have to learn to walk barefoot. Sometimes I see people walking around barefoot while I am out camping, and they can barely walk on their soft feet. The world has many different ways of life: the old, the new, and the future. No matter what others are doing around you, it is the most important to remain true to who you are and respect your happiness and beliefs.

As for myself, I have experienced a diverse life filled with travel and rich culture. Introduced to various indigenous elders from Native American, South American and African American tribes. I have also visited His Holiness the 14th Dalai Lama and a well-know woman in India, Amma, known as the hugging saint. One of my clients came in to get a massage from me in 2006 and invited me to go to Colorado with her to see the His Holiness the 14th Dalai Lama at a new temple located near the Red Feather Mountains. I drove my two-door sports car through the mountains covered with snow to our hotel the evening before he was flying in. Before sunrise the next day, we drove up to the temple where vans took us closer from the parking area; then we walked in the freezing cold up the path. By the time His Holiness the 14th Dalai Lama arrived in a helicopter, there were thousands of people waiting to greet him. When I was getting dressed in the morning to go see him, I wanted to wear my buckskin dress, but I was too worried about what other people might think about it. So, instead, I wore regular American clothes with a hat and coat because it was very cold that early morning in the mountains. When people started to arrive, I noticed that there were women from different tribes that came to light sage and medicines on the stage and they were all in their buckskin regalia. I was very disappointed in myself, for not listening to my inner voice to wear my buckskin dress.

When I traveled to Dallas, TX, to see Mata Amritanandamayi Devi (Amma from Kerala, India), I did wear my buckskin dress. Then, when I went again in 2012, I wore my traditional dress again. My close friend that travels with Amma told me that Amma liked that I wore my buckskin dress to see her. I think it is respectful to wear your traditional clothes to honor your relatives and ancestors who look over you, as well as a respected person such as Mata Amritanandamayi Devi and His Holiness the 14th Dalai Lama whom help so many people on this planet. It makes the people on earth happy and your families in other dimensions smile to see you passing on traditions. It also just feels wonderfully pleasant to have that soft deerskin covering my skin.

Because my life is so multi-faceted, I have spent hundreds of hours doing laundry! I have to wear my black suit and heels to the office downtown, then come home and put on some exercise clothes to clean up or take a walk. I'm changing into my massage clothes with my shirt with my business name on it to look professional for that job, then I'm changing into my dress for Inipi ceremony or a skirt for prayer ceremony at night. By the end of most days, I would wear over five different outfits! When you practice being yourself and dressing how you feel most comfortable, you do not think about how everyone else wants to see you. Although there may be dress codes at work, there are not dress codes for going to the store or to the movies. Take time to create your appearance that feels most like you.

When I am doing healing work on someone and notice that one of their energy centers, or chakras, need work, I will let them know to wear that specific color to help them balance. Sometimes we may need to wear certain colors to help uplift our moods or help our energy balance out, but we are afraid to look silly to other people. Oftentimes when I mention to someone what color they need to wear more, they tell me that it's their favorite color to wear. Specific colors of clothing will help to uplift your moods, especially if you have to wear black at work or suits all of the time. The clothes that you wear have an effect on your emotions and personality.

When I substituted in elementary and middle schools, I would wear suits to keep the attention of the children in the classroom and make sure they would listen to me. As a teacher, I am strong and confident to keep the children's attention, yet I am kind and patient at the same time. I may wear traditional clothes when I am a "spiritual teacher," speaking to groups of people my age or older. Then, I am wise and confident and strong. There is always a different dress code or "personality codes." There are dresses for fine-dining and for meetings and interviews.

Not that I didn't enjoy going to business meetings and events all of the time; I was just tired of doing so much laundry and trying to impress everyone else! I was so wrapped up in what others thought about me that I didn't even know what I liked to wear or what was comfortable to me at the time. Not that I don't enjoy dressing up or wearing suits; it's just that I felt pressured to look or act a certain way, and I had to realize that I wasn't being myself. I realized just how uncomfortable with myself that I really was.

It was amazing once I had this realization. I got rid of bags and bags of clothes, and whatever I tried on that didn't feel like "me," I gave away to my family and friends or the thrift store. I also realized that some of the clothes were attachment clothes and I never wore but kept them for memories that I didn't want to lose. I also noticed how I wore certain clothes because they were similar to my friends, or the current fashion. I wore the haircuts, did my make up like magazines—and whatever I thought I needed to apply to fit in. Being myself and throwing away the masks that were not me have been one of my hardest challenges. I never really thought of myself as wearing a mask and not being myself, but I came to realize, I was wearing many, and many of them were not my truth. It's not that you only have one mask to wear, but that you are wearing your own, and not someone else's. Think of a mask as a talent, gift, or a certain personality. We have more than one personality and more than one gift; it's only that you need to see that the masks you wear are yours and you accept the one's that you are wearing. The main point is to know that whatever mask you are wearing is one that is true to you and the one that you want to show to the world around you.

Time to be Honest with Yourself

Are you comfortable with yourself (body, attitudes, location)?

_____

_____

_____

_____

Is this your true self?

_____

_____

_____

_____

Are you concerned with what others think?

_____

_____

_____

_____

Does what you are doing in life make you happy, or just done to make others happy?

_____

_____

_____

_____

When we are concerned with what others think about us, it can easily take us off of our truth path, the path that is true to us. We are not here to live someone else's life or to fulfill someone else's dream for them; we are here to fulfill our own dreams and to walk in our beauty. It is when we recognize how much we allow what others think to deflect us from our path, can we start to put our foot down and take a stand for ourselves and let our own lights shine. It is only then that you will realize who you really are and allow your full potential to come forth, your full presence with all of your beauty, strengths, and talents that you have to share with everyone.

One of the biggest impacts of wearing masks of others that I have seen in families is "tradition" and "religion". I hear parents and elders telling their children and others to learn their traditional ways. But first, you have to know what tradition means to *that* person. Tradition could be from five-hundred years ago, or recently from their grandparents. Tradition can mean different things to different people, so make sure you respect that we all have different meanings of what tradition is. Some traditions that are passed down are the way we prepare food; from how we plant it, crop it, harvest it, cook it, and serve it. Other ways that are passed down can be the way that we dress, our mannerisms, family structures, and even how we view life. What traditions we learn from our family are how most of us see our experiences in the world around us. You may feel like others are doing everything wrong, because they are not doing it the same way that you were taught. In my tribe, there are many old traditions where a woman and a man play different roles in ceremonies and this is still acted out on my reservation.

The most important thing to ask yourself is what feels right to you? Then, ask that person what does tradition mean to them, and see how they are living their life. See if they are taking care of themselves well and treating others with love and respect. I noticed how one elder was telling me that I should not play the drum or flute because I am a woman, and I thought to myself, well you are driving a car and living in a house, how traditional is that? The most important thing in finding teachers, guides, and helpers is to see how they resonate with your *feelings* and beliefs. Just because someone is related to you by blood does not necessarily mean that you are meant to follow in their footsteps. Some religions and traditions included sacrificing children, women, or animals, as well as other rituals which mostly have been banned during recent years. If you were raised in a strong religious family or one with long traditions, it may take more time to discover your true self and to make sure you are on your right path.

It is so important to be yourself because otherwise, you are missing out being alive and not only for yourself, but also for the many others who will cross your path in this lifetime. If you are hiding and pretending to be something you are not, then you will be attracting people and experiences that are pretend as well, and keep you from your path. You will attract what and who you are living, and it will stay that way until you decide to take off your masks and open up your voice, your heart, and shine your beautiful light with the world around you. So, being yourself may sound pretty simple to you, and to some of you it sounds like a life-long journey. Remember, we all have a different path, each unique, and special; and the only judge is you.

The experiences that you have learned in this lifetime I view as schoolbooks and classes. Let's say that life is a school; sometimes you have to keep enrolling for the same class over and over until you learn and grow from the experience. Sometimes our teachers and leaders teach us what not to do, and sometimes they teach us what to do. That is why we have our intuition and gut feelings to ask our inner selves, or higher self. Is the situation or lesson that I am in serving my highest good? Sometimes we make decisions based on fear and illusion which tend to be the easier path. When you are learning to be yourself, be ready to accept changes and your experiences as teachings in a book at school.

When you are done judging yourself, no one else can judge you. And when you fully accept and love yourself, everyone else will accept you and love you too! And those people you come across that you feel jealousy or anger from, then you send them love and shine your light; it is their choice to open up and receive the love you shine, or not. When you fully accept yourself and live life as yourself, many new people, places, and choices will appear. You will sense the freedom that life has to offer you, and you will be more open to the ever-changing flow of life. When the love of life is flowing freely through you, you will love everyone and everything around you. You may see only into your highest light and truth, and this in turn, will help others to see themselves in their highest light and truth.

This is what helping yourself does; it automatically helps

others. I am not saying that everyone needs to be aware of helping others, or needs to, but, if you are interested, here are some of my thoughts and personal experiences. I welcome you to try this exercise of love wherever you go: when you see someone walking by, look them in the eyes and say hello. Do not look down, or away, but greet them with a smile and say, 'hello." A few weeks ago, I was visiting a friend in Lawrence who was teaching a yoga class and we had gone to a grocery store after class. I looked at the young lady at the checkout stand in the eyes and said with a smile, "Hello, I love you," and she looked at me and said, "I love you too!" We were all standing there with heartfelt smiles and huge overflowing hearts. It was a beautiful moment, and I was so excited that she said she loved me back! Every now and then if I tell someone I love them, they will simply say thank you and smile. And then, years down the road, they will say I love you too.

Every time you are near someone you are sharing and exchanging energy and spiritual connections, and if someone is "having a bad day," then their energy field is not going to feel so welcoming and calming, but if they are "on top of the world,", floating around in heaven on earth, then you are going to love to be around them and be a part of their life. When I feel like I am full and overflowing with love, I will ask people that I see if they would like a hug, and most of them are so happy that you asked for a hug! Life is so amazing and beautiful, yet it's hard to see it and experience it when you are caught up in the mind of yourself and of others. If you feel called to, then please try some of your own ways to share love with yourself and others. You will not believe how far a smile or a warm hug will go.

And most importantly, when working on being yourself, remember to always be grateful for all of your experiences. Oftentimes, we are afraid to change, not because of ourselves, but in fear of hurting others feelings. It is also good to thank and give gratitude to your parents and grandparents every day and other relatives (descendents) up to seven generations. This helps to clear up any anger, pain, resentment, or hurtful feelings that you or your relatives might be experiencing. It is not important to know your biological parents or ancestors. It is important, however, to honor them by thanking them each day. This will also help to clear out any pain or abuse that you may have experienced in this lifetime, or past lifetimes.

CHAPTER SIX

₪ Follow Your Dream

"All we are is the result of what we have thought."

~Buddha~

In this world we have two sides. We have simplicity and difficulty. However, don't let the word "simplicity" fool you. Simple things are often the hardest to complete. Hard things that that may sound simple are finishing school, learning to drive, or starting a new relationship. Things in life become not so simple because difficult things have happened in our life that causes the simple things to appear hard. For some of us, just enjoying life or time with yourself or your family is a hard task to do. For others, being difficult all of the time is a normal, everyday schedule. I like the analogy that each of us has a black wolf and a white wolf within, and it's up to us which one we are going to feed.

In some of the spiritual training I have had, the teacher would have us to name the different parts of ourselves, and then make sure that we pay them attention. For example, if you have a funny side, an angry side, and an artistic side; make sure that you are spending time with each of them, in order to keep harmony within. The natural world is complex, yet simple in the fact that it simply flows continuously in cycles. Within the human mind is where we have difficulty. It is the power of the mind that can stop the flow, make currents and uproars, and build bridges and walls. Then, it is up to us to allow those bridges that we built to work, or for them to come crashing down destroying what we have tried to build. Sometimes procrastination or fear can break down a bridge, or collapse a wall. Or perhaps, we neglect our project all together.

Perhaps, you created plans for your future, and then had an unexpected child. Maybe you started a new relationship and completely forgot all about your project or dream that you had created for the last five years of your life. When you create a dream in your mind, you are actually bringing in energy within your consciousness, and energy field around you.

Therefore, if you decide to change your dream or venture, begin to inform or transform all that you have already created. You may want to place the energy of your dream to your child, or perhaps you just want to put it on hold. You may say, "Energy of this dream of traveling the world, I now am going to apply this energy to my beautiful child!" Perhaps, you had a dream book of all the places you were going to go soon, or maybe even a savings account. Whatever you chose to do, you need to let the energy of the pursuit be known. Perhaps, you may even want to give it away if you have manifested any of it in the material world (maybe you had plane tickets already).

Here's an example: you want to own your own beauty salon and you purchase five thousand dollars worth of salon equipment and place it in storage. Now, after five years of thinking that you could never get pregnant, you get pregnant! You decide that you want to take care of your child yourself and do not have the time to run a salon. Instead of keeping everything in storage for a few years, you decide to either sell the furniture to someone else, or have a relative that you trust run the salon for you. You always have options when you begin or change a dream, but it is important to respect that dream and follow through with some sort of closure (even closure through transformation).

The follow through on whatever choice you make is the key elemental. What I see people doing the most is not doing anything at all out of fear of failure. If you do nothing, or if you decide to try something new and fail, either way you are failing; but if you try, you are gaining closure! This closure means you have actually gained and reclaimed your energy and learned a lesson. Now that you have "failed," you can move on to the next several options or dreams that are now open and even more advanced than the last.

A dream is like a life or a baby that you nurture and spend lots of time thinking about and planning the future. Each time you think about something, you are feeding it and nursing life to it. This is why I say in one of my chapters, do not blame it; claim it! Remember, whatever or whoever your thoughts are focusing on is where your energy is being sent.

I remember one day I was at the hospital with one of my nephews who used to have leukemia, and while sitting in the waiting room, I saw a famous talk-show host over in Africa giving boy's balls and girl's dolls to play with. Tears came flooding down my face as I saw one of my visions taking place. This is an example of what our thoughts can do. It reminds me of what some people call prayers. They are good thoughts, daydreams, or perhaps even your dreams when you sleep that are manifested in the material world we live in.

When I was a child, I began to have nightmares. They were always about a monster under my bed, or hiding in the house, or even chasing me down the street. I was always trying to run, but I couldn't. I was always trying to ride my tricycle, and he would get close, and I would wake up. So, one day, one of my greatest teachers and healers, my mother, simply tells me, "just stop and turn around and tell him firmly," "this is my dream!" "Leave me alone!" And you know what? It worked! That monster just stopped in his big furry tracks and looked at me. He wasn't even scary or mean. He just stopped and never bothered me again. Ever since then, I started studying about dreams and the dream world.

I learned that it is very empowering to be able to look at yourself in a mirror while you are sleeping. Being able to know that you are in a dream is called "lucid dreaming." For several months I kept losing my teeth in my dreams while I was looking in a bathroom mirror. To me, it was like "trying to pull teeth" to be able to look at myself! But one day, I looked in a mirror, and I was perfectly fine. Then after I accomplished that, a different teacher taught me to look at my hands in a dream, and after sometime, I was able to do that too.

I spent many years flying and traveling in my dreams. I went to Paris and climbed the Eifel tower and jumped off with a parachute. Then I flew through the deserts in Arizona and the four corners. I went to different places that I wanted to see and practiced visiting my friends that I no longer talk to. One in particular was my best friend Suzzie who I lost contact with several years ago due to family issues and miss dearly. My family moved to Salina, KS for a couple of years my last year of middle school and I met Suzzie, and we were inseparable right away. I spent most of my nights at her house and we did everything together. And then, my best friend Ashley who took the Journey over ten years ago. After living in Salina for two years, then Newton for another year, I moved back to Wichita with my family and was reunited with Ashley in High school. She was my best friend from the fourth grade before we moved away. When I found out that she had passed away in a car accident I was so devastated that I did not leave my apartment for about a week (not even to go to her funeral). I didn't call her mother, or even visit her gravesite for ten years. So, when I started working with my dreams, I went to go see her all the time. I was always sad or crying and finally, Ashley told me that she was ok and to stop worrying about her.

When I was a little girl, before I started doing dream-work, I heard and felt spirits and saw auras around myself and other people. I helped people and spirits by clearing any negative or stuck energy in their homes. I freed the earthbound spirits that had material or family ties to the physical world. I found a lot of the spirits who had a hard time releasing their loved ones that were still alive. I started doing this around 1988, and I still practice house clearing to this day, as well as land clearing and body clearing of void energies.

As I started being more aware of my dreams, I started noticing people that I worked on, friends, family, and children I have never seen before, but I knew they existed as I started meeting some of them a few months later. Sometimes when a friend stayed the night, I would experience what it was like inside their minds, hearts, and spirits; and sometimes they would ask me to help them, and I would be in their "house" and see all of their thoughts, turmoil, and things that they were holding on to or not forgiving themselves or someone else for. I could see people that had passed away that they were still missing and in pain. I could see experiences that had recently caused them suffering.

Dreams are a powerful way on earth to assist you in following your purpose and your life path. A dream can be a great expansion of the minds vast imagination, and a dream can be a map of your past, present, and future experiences. I think that those who believe in themselves can follow their dreams; my only rule is that whatsoever dream you choose to follow will not harm you or another living being. In a literal sense, I do believe that the dreams you have in the dream state are often signs and memories of the past. The dreams may also be of the future, and when applied as a tool, they can be very helpful in guiding you on your path.

Do you ever wonder why you have certain desires or goals? What if you don't have an aspiration, or your ideas may be your parents' dream that you feel like you have to fulfill in order for them to live through you in a sense. First, make sure that your dream(s) is yours and that it comes right from your heart. Then, what are you waiting for? Hmm…ok. The first thing that comes to mind is money. What in the world is that? Some people think money is everything, and some people think that money is power. Some people associate money with sex, love, and happiness. So, let's go back a few chapters now. What is your attachment to money and why? Where does that stem from? Ok, let's lovingly release these attachments and stories that you have to money and understand that money is itself its own energy and can now be accepted in your life to follow your dreams. Remember, when you believe, anything is possible all you have to do is follow your heart.

The helpful dream world has helped me attain my dreams here on earth as well. My adventurous dreams gave me the confidence I needed to start living my dreams here. I moved away when I was nineteen years old for a fresh start in life. It was a hard move, leaving all of my friends and my old ways of life behind. I found a job that led to even more growth and confidence. I was a teenager managing up to fifty people for my office. It was only a temporary job, so that made it much more relaxing. On the last week, with about my last ten or fifteen crew left, I made everyone Indian tacos and had a celebration. One man brought his guitar and he sang us the blues. We took pictures and wore party necklaces and had a gay, merry time. After that job was completed, I moved back to Wichita and my old job testing computer chips. It was about a month later when I decided to quit and work for my mother doing massages again.

After about six months, a man came in to get a massage and was a teacher of anesthesiology. He came in town from Texas to give a lecture. He was amazed by my energy work and spirit communication and said that I would be perfect as a Nurse Anesthetist. At the time, I had no idea what this was, and, as a matter of fact, I didn't even make it through high-school, but I did receive my Diploma right before I moved back to Wichita. So, that same week, I enrolled at Wichita State University and started school two weeks later in the summer. Going to college was very intimidating to me, and I thought that was going to fail. I was fifteen years old when I stopped going to school and had tried three different high schools. Each had various problems, and I never felt like I fit in.

My first high-school that I went to, I was called names for being "Native American Indian" and was attacked more than once by other students. The day that I decided to leave my first high-school was because a boy had called me names and decided to start hitting me in math class. When I went to the office there was another fight in the parking lot, so I decided to go home and never return. About two weeks into classes at my second high-school that I enrolled in, there were two girls fighting over a boy and one stabbed the other one, resulting in death. So then, I enrolled in a third high-school. The third one was a metro school for kids that were kicked out of normal schools. There I experienced sexual harassment, more drugs, and verbal abuse, just like all the other schools I attended. I completed some of my English classes, record-keeping, and math and then I opted out of school altogether. After I had dropped out of high-school, I didn't really have a desire to finish school, but I did want to get my diploma and attend a college in Lawrence, KS that was for enrolled tribal members only.

When I moved to Topeka in 1999, I finished my high-school diploma, and therefore, I was able to attend WSU right away. As the weeks went by, I realized how much I enjoyed school. I loved all the different people, writing papers, and attending different school clubs and meetings. Every semester I made the dean's honor roll and I graduated with my Associates Degree with Honors. I had chosen

Nursing as my major and Women Studies and Entrepreneurship as my minor. My dreams of being successful were coming true!

During finals week, I got a call from my mother. Since I was taking a test and couldn't answer, she left me a message. It said, "Our appointments canceled today, and I don't think its working out." and she had to let me go. So, with tears in my eyes and wonder in my heart, I took back her key to the office and left it in the mailbox. This was the beginning of my new business, Massage Made Convenient. I decided to start going to people's homes and offered massages out of my apartment at the time. School was a lot of work and time and I marketed on the campus to try to make ends meet.

Almost two years went by, and I was struggling in my four-year long-relationship with a long-time friend. We had rented a house together, and I was not supported going to school. I had to stay up late doing my homework and getting up early for school. My massage business had picked up, and I wanted to open my own office, but I was not supported in that either. I had just graduated with my Associate's Degree and was starting my first semester towards my Bachelors degree. I felt myself coming unraveled, and then one day while in lab biology, I got another disappointing message from my mom on my cell phone. The message said, "Uncle passed away; they found him in his car." That day I had called one of my uncle's sons' to come help me move out of my house. I decided to end the relationship that was not supporting my needs of school, work, and love. I left my classroom right away and headed to my

117

uncle's home. I felt shortness of breath and thought I was dying on the highway. I later realized it was only an anxiety attack. I helped pack up my uncle's apartment for a couple of hours and then headed home to pack up my own.

I moved out of my home, dropped out of school, and opened my first massage office in Wichita. I had three rooms with a front room, as well as my own office space back behind the desk in a separate room. I worked for three years there expanding my office from three rooms to six and started teaching and holding drumming circles. I had a few other massage therapists working there with me including my mother. I really enjoyed spending a lot of time at work and I was always learning and growing in relationships and studies. My life was looking up, and I couldn't believe the changes that were happening so fast.

After about two years went by, I started getting phone calls from different healers around the world wanting to meet me and made new friends when they visited Wichita. Some day's people would walk in off the streets and offer me healing work and share their stories with me of medicine and healing. I was gifted with many tools from teachers to help me on my journey. I was beginning to live my dream and it was materializing without a doubt. I started making a lot of money, and I didn't have plans for it all because I thought this could not happen to me! I ended up giving to friends and family and would always be broke. I started helping the homeless out once a month and doing lots of free work. Then that's when I decided that I needed a more solid plan; I need a foundation; I needed me.

I had started a new relationship with an entire family of six and all of my time and money was spent with them more and less at work. I felt like I was getting lost and unraveling again, so I removed myself from this relationship after three years in 2007. I moved out only days before going on a journey to Guatemala for Trance Dance Facilitator training. This was the beginning of me finally concentrating on myself. I saw this as time to face my fears, my passions, my desires, and take a look at who I was and where I was heading in life.

And that's how my dream came to be. I finished with another beautiful chapter of my life and always saw the doors to limitless new beginnings. As sure as there is life on earth, when one door closes, there will be several more waiting for you to choose.

Following your dreams is not always as it seems in the dream world. There are steps to follow requiring perseverance and work. But it is always those small, magical moments that prove the dream to be well worth it! I have made a list of things that I am now open to receive on my path, and if you do not have a list, I strongly suggest writing a list or making a vision board. A vision board is very fun and helpful for processing your dreams into a reality. I have been making these for many years, and I even enjoy updating them on occasion. I often make small ones on water coloring paper with magazines and after a few short years, everything in the pictures has come to actualization. Then, I have the larger ones that I keep that may show things revealed in about 10 to 15 more years! All you need are some poster board, some magazine or markers, cut out pictures, and words. I like to put pictures of myself on there, or even just a picture of my face to show where I want to be in life. I have applied pictures of the mountains; getting a massage; traveling the world; the water being clean and pure; and writing in words to state what I want to accept into my life. When you have some spare time for yourself, write down these words and what each one means to you. This will help you to find some pictures for your vision board, even if you are drawing them out with a crayon or marker. You may also choose to use feathers, beads, chalk or anything else to express your being and your fullest potential! Be as creative as you can and have fun with this!

Here is an example of things that you can write down stating out loud: "I Am open to receive:"

I Am Open to Receive…

Love & Compassion

Abundance

Truth & Respect

Wisdom & Knowledge

Fun with New Experiences

Travel with Joy & Inspiration

Excitement

Joy

New opportunities

Grace

Messages from my Spirit

Messages from my Soul

Messages from the Water

Messages from my Body Elemental

Messages from my Ancestors

Beautiful Gifts

Guidance & Protection

Messages from my Guides

Love from inside & All Around Me

Open Communication with All Beings of Light

CHAPTER SEVEN

₪ Continue to Grow

"Just plant the seed and let it grow. If you dig it up with doubt every day, you have to start from scratch again tomorrow."

~ Crystal D. Gingras ~

In order to write this book to disclose, I had to include a lot of my own personal and very private experiences. Continuing to grow is an enormous part of the work on earth for me. It's currently 4:50 a.m., and I am up reading a book by a medium (one who talks to the deceased). I am sitting here asking my spirit guides and angels for guidance and protection. Also, I am connecting to mother earth and sending any lower energy safely to the core of the earth to be transmuted back to the circle of life. Focusing on my room being filled with a golden ball of light and expanding out to the universe, I felt a strong urge to pick up my laptop and begin writing again. I always wish that these words would all just flow out of me, but it seems like writing this book has really helped me describe my actions, my life, and also the changes that I am experiencing.

I hear how people want to write a book, but they don't because they say that everything has already been written. Well, if you believe in the circle, the spiral, or the endless, limitless space, then everything has been done before; but we are still here, living the dream! I say, go for what your heart desires and only listen to your own inner truth. I used to wish that this book would just "flow out of me," as if it were channeled, but then I remembered that everything is meant to be just as it is. Sometimes, when you read a book, you may very well already know everything that you are reading, but just needed a reminder. Also, the most important thing about reading books, or learning from writers or teachers, is that two different teachers may teach the exact same thing, word for word, but it's the essence of the person that distinguishes the two.

It's all about the connection with the other person. It's similar to what I learned at the age of twelve when I took my first Reiki class. My Reiki manual said that not all teachers are the same, and some are more powerful than others. I look at teachers being equally powerful, but that the experience of being taught by one over the other is greater if it's the right teacher. I look at the books the same way as teachers, in that with every word that is written by a certain writer will have a different result for each reader.

To continue to grow means that you are recognizing your potential and choosing to grow into what you see. I believe that as long as you are still alive on earth, then, my relative, you still have work to do! To continue to grow and follow your instincts and your heart is important. Stay focused on trusting your intuition, and allow yourself to relax and enjoy your time on earth. There are many opportunities and signs around us all of the time, and once you open up to acceptance and support, they will become easier to see. The most important thing now is to take your time to develop a natural flow that works for you. Always remember that we are each unique; therefore, we each have different areas for growth as well as different areas for growth, as well as different seasons for change and relaxation.

As you may have noticed, I really enjoy inspirational quotes and have put them at the beginning of each chapter. There is one popular quote by Nike, "Just Do It," that reminds us that everything we need is already right there; everything. If you are supposed to do something now, then all that you need is already provided. There are some safety issues that may be involved so please use your common sense and always take your time in any new adventure as you grow. The key to change is perseverance and patients, hence, taking it slow.

The medicine of the turtle is to walk slowly, yet when needed to, can run very fast! I remember once when I took my niece to the park and there was a turtle that she was following down the path we were walking. When she got up close, the turtle took off running very fast, and she screamed in surprise that turtles can run! I say the word "medicine" because there is something to taking it slowly. Medicine is something that helps you to grow, or bring you back to balance and harmony. When you look at time, I mean really deep into time, you can study it for a whole lifetime by digging deeply into quantum physics, quantum jumping, worm holes, past lives, reincarnation, etc. Some people will flat out say that there is no time, and, therefore, when you "take your time" means that you are following your path. When you are rushing, it is usually for a job or work, or you are going to be late. You begin to worry about the "time-clock," or maybe you are going to disappoint someone or worry about missing something. I heard an elder say once that when you are following your truth path, you begin to slow down and really live in the moment. You take time to see, feel, hear, smell, and experience life in a completely different way. You notice the small things in life around you that you have never noticed before. Your senses will begin to improve vastly, including your intuition, hearing, sight and feelings. This growing sensitivity affects not only yourself, but, also all others around you. When you are in the hustle and bustle of everyday life, you block out your inner-self and the beauty of the world around you. Only when you slow down can you really live and fulfill your destiny.

About ten years ago, I was going to write this book to talk

about all of the ceremonies that I have attended, the great teachers I had as a child, the spirits that I helped cross over to the light as a child, and everything that I had experienced in my life. I was going to share all of my physical, emotional, and sexual abuse I knew growing up and how it relates to what is happening to Mother Earth. We are reflections of each other and the earth and the elements show us reflections of what we do to ourselves. What we do to ourselves, we do to each other and to the earth. When it was time to finish my book, I reached a place in my life where I only shared my thoughts and focused on my higher self. I decided that my thoughts and words had power as I saw many things manifesting faster and faster. I knew that it was time to keep growing at a more peaceful and healthy pace instead of riding huge waves up and down which included lots of unnecessary pain and suffering.

The elements--the earth, the wind, the water, and the fire--are all apart of us as well, so not only can you see your reflection in another human being, but also you can see the earth and your reflection. I decided to change the name of my book from *The Rape of Mother Earth* to *Time Is Running Out* because that always seemed important in my dreams and visions when I hear or feel messages about how important this book is. Continual growth is learning to trust your inner voice and follow it no matter what or who is around. Learn to listen to your instincts and your guides to assist you to follow your path, your destiny, and the reasons why you chose to be born. There are many different paths to follow in this lifetime, which means that there are many different tools to help you grow spiritually,

and this book is just one of them. When you are listening to your
inner voice that means you are in alignment with your higher self or
the divine, and this happens when you learn to trust.

At times, I like to share this story that occurred during one of
my meditations. Approximately three years ago during meditation, I
visualized a radiant golden skin-toned boy slowly walking towards
me. I gazed around us and observed nothing but beautiful soft white
sand and clear blue waters. The soft and pink sunrise was glistening
beside us on the left as he arrived in front of me. This small radiant
being was dressed in a leather breechcloth the color of elk-hide and
had dark brown hair and striking golden eyes. As he knelt down
before me, he dug a little hole and put a seed in there and stared into
my eyes and said, "Mom, don't dig this up." I simply said, "Ok," and
after that, he turned away and disappeared into the morning sun.

Around that time I thought I was pregnant, but I found out
some things about the father that I decided that I could not live with
and prayed that I wasn't pregnant. I told the child that it wasn't the
right father and I couldn't conceive. For a few months I felt guilty,
but then I thought, who really knows if I was pregnant or not!
Perhaps the whole situation and symptoms were completely inside
my head. However, I generally trust my inner voice! In May of 2008,
I went to a course for my massage practice on applying essential oils
to the body, and when I arrived one of my friends I've known since
childhood was there. She's a psychic, and we used to work at the
same Spiritual Fairs together. She would do readings, and I either did

readings of energy and auras or massages for people. She and I were talking, and she asked if she could tell me something. I said yes, sure. She said you recently had a miscarriage and needed to hear that. I cried immediately and told her what I had done. I felt so bad for turning away my own child and just the thought seemed silly at the time, but as I write this, it still brings tears to my eyes. I am so blessed to have been at this class of healers and helpers. They all put some oils and their loving hands on me to help release the hurt as I wept. I believe that I wanted a child so badly, but wasn't the right time yet. I was pushing for a child with whomever I was dating and not letting things flow with divine order. I took responsibility for my thoughts and recognized what I was doing. Right away, I asked for forgiveness and released the trauma, although it was a very agonizing experience.

I have noticed that when you continue to grow, life changes all the time. The people around you change, jobs change, and your home life may even change. I believe that as you are growing to be your highest self, then naturally the environment around you will shift to match that higher self. Sometimes people around you are not finished with their lesson or experience, or that part of your experience together is over, so they move on. Someone else on a different level or bringing a new experience will arrive. This is one of the reasons why attachments are so negative and on a lower vibration because often time's attachments can become destructive and detrimental.

I contemplated not writing down any negative words of

experiences or feelings, but it's challenging to explain to someone without looking at the other components. For example, as a holistic life coach, I find it extremely helpful to contain the experience of physical and emotional suffering in my lifetime to facilitate relating to clients. I see the past experiences as a worthy understanding to relate to others. To be aware of the "dark side," disease, or negative experiences, enables you to recognize it in others and help them move away from that pattern. Whenever I sense an old thought pattern, I simply acknowledge the thought, thank it, and honor the experience. Then, utilizing imagination and visualization, I call upon Archangel Michael and my higher consciousness to send any lower frequencies and "old stories" that are no longer serving my highest good or soul's purpose up to the light.

I began my foundation of natural medicine in early childhood. I started attending ceremonies with my mother around the age of one. I would go to Inipi (sweat lodge) ceremonies, Sundance, and moon ceremonies with her. Around the age of ten, I attended workshops with her in different states with our teacher Oh Shinnah and some others in different states. Before I was old enough, I would attend a Spiritualist Church camp every summer, and the managers would allow me to join the teenager's camp which was held right before the adult camp. We would practice psychometry and have séances and other spiritual classes.

One of my teachers was a Tai Chi instructor, and he was unsympathetic! One by one, he had each of us come after him to choke him, and on the way towards him, he would place his hands together to build his chi (life force energy). As we got near him, he would direct his hands at us and knock us on the ground. He continued to do this practice to every student there. Then, one of the spiritual teachers at the camp from Denton, TX got up to test his chi level with him (this teacher was very intuitive and was able to move objects and communicate with the spirit world. I stayed with him and his wife during my summer school breaks to learn more). My teacher had put his hands around this man's neck and was squeezing with all his strength and I remember both of their faces were turning red and I remember someone had to stop them from killing each other! To me, that was an experience of ego trying to be more powerful than someone else and show off. I can still remember feeling confused and embarrassed by the whole situation.

I also wonder if some spirits don't like you to curse because one of my friends who talks to spirits frequently told me that the spirits get nervous when I cuss. I can understand this, because when I see a friend cussing, I wonder what darkness is surrounding them. As a teenager, at the Spiritual Camp that I attended, one of the guys there was walking in front of the church cursing, and this spirit flew right out of a brick wall on the church and knocked him right off his feet! We all immediately knew why! He saw the spirit fly right off the stones on the church wall and knock him down. I spent a good three summers there at least, and I was honored that they allowed me to stay even before I was thirteen years old. I was pretty young when I started praying to the spirits every night, asking who needed help crossing over to the light. I would call on their trusted relatives who could comfort them through this transition. The entire room would fill up with earthbound spirits and I would start sending them over to the light if they were ready. Sometimes I would think that the spirits might give me mysteries to solve, or some adventure.

I never did experience a ghost adventure, until one day, when my sister and her friends were playing the Ouija board, and she brought a lower energy spirit home. He seemed to attach to me right away, and I started having bad dreams. He had followed me in my dreams pretending to be my father. He was always dressed up in black suits and wore a black hat. I think he pretended to be my father, because my father was not in my life, and that's what caused me so much sadness and pain. In my bedroom at home, he would turn on the radio that I unplugged and play parts of scary songs to scare me at night. He was also daunting my sister's friends who were present that night with my sister. He bothered my sister and me for about a year or two. Around the summer of 1992, I was at the Sunset Spiritualist Camp. This angry ghost who had been haunting me started to move things in my room. The closet doors were slamming, my bed was shaking, and I built up enough courage to make it off of my bed and run to tell the staff.

We went to the small séance room at the camp, and they had everyone else go inside of the church and did not tell them what was going on. I remember at least three people sitting in there with me to help hold space. The staff sat in each corner of the room to ground the energy and then one sat next to me at a table, and then Hallie (the one that I stayed in Texas with), that did spirit communication sat in the middle.

There was always a dim red light bulb lit in there that was turned on as we entered the room. She called on Archangel Michael and the other Arch Angels. Then, she called on this spirit that was just attacking me in my cabin room by his name. I knew his name from his visits and from when he was brought through the Ouija board years before. He immediately showed up when she called his name and then all of a sudden I had pain in my hands and felt a strong presence from him in the physical world as if he was attacking me. She started to pray loud to the Angels to take him to the Light and the person beside me was holding tight onto my right arm. Then I saw two Angels beside him and he was wearing shackles around his ankles and his wrists. The Angels were on each sides of him with their hands on his arms guiding him on this staircase up to a very bright light. He looked back at me and said in a mean voice, "I'll be back," and I replied, "No, you won't." As soon as he left and went to the Light, I felt one hundred percent better. I learned from all those years of him haunting me and torturing me in my dreams and in real life to never play with the Ouija board, so I have never used it as a medium to communicate.

Over the years I continued to do house blessing, and I currently do them whenever I am asked. The person in need usually finds me through a random interaction with me or someone that I know. Sometimes they are friends, or someone my mother knows, or a client of mine. I was at a conference a few weeks ago in Phoenix, and there were several people there who communicated with the spirit world as well as angels. I was thinking to myself that I wanted to communicate more as a means to help others out. And so, the next day at the conference, I had a beautiful experience in class with an eighty-year old woman. We were doing some work together in a group with that particular teacher, and afterwards I gave her a kiss on the cheek. Right when I kissed her cheek, we both felt the strong vibration of love and tingles. Several moments later while we were sitting and listening to the speaker in that class, I automatically placed my left arm around her shoulders in endearment. I will usually hug people that I talk to if I feel that they are open to it. Also, if I am sitting in class and feel that someone is in need of love, healing or touch, I will first ask them, "May I touch you?". However, this was different. This was a stranger that I smiled and said hello to and then I would normally just sit there and pay attention to class but something different was happening. Something divine and meaningful.

As I had my arm around her shoulder, she was holding my hand, and I felt so much love flowing through us and around us that my eyes started to water. I sensed her husband was there who had passed away two years prior. She told me earlier that they had been married for sixty years and that's why she had come there to move forward from his death. While my arm was around her, the movie "Ghost" came to mind, so I asked if she liked that movie and she said it was her favorite, and she mentioned the part about the pottery. Then I said, did your husband used to put his arm around you like this, and she replied "all the time." We both got the chills then and earlier when I kissed her on the cheek. When I get the chills or goose bumps, which is the indicator of how I know a spirit is there working through someone or around us. For example, when someone is relaying a story or memory, I will get chills for a confirmation that it is a real story or the correct person in spirit that they are talking about.

Class was still going on, and everyone was clapping, so I removed my arm and started clapping too. Then I thought to myself, why didn't I ask for a confirmation, as if it wasn't enough already; so I heard the voice whisper, "I'm still here". A wooden box with pearl earrings came to mind, so I told her about that and she knew for sure that it was her husband there with her through me. She was so excited, and we were filled with so much love that we exchanged phone numbers and addresses to stay in touch. I have always enjoyed growth and learning, but right now I keep getting the message to just relax, spend some time for myself, and enjoy life for a bit, and allow this new information to soak in.

I do believe that is very important to allow yourself to take the time to let new information integrate into the human system. I also believe that you have to take care of yourself first and foremost before you can really take care of anyone else. I also realized when writing this book and sharing tips for people to start working on themselves that I still need to complete some of what I have to communicate. I used to feel I could not teach or share anything until I had completed or mastered it. But now, I know that some things aren't meant for me to master, but they are very important for me to share with others. I realized that I was human, and so are other humans, and that we will always be a work in progress because that's exactly why we are here on earth.

I was getting worked on by a lady once who mentioned how she doesn't write a book because everything is already out there anyway and there's already enough information. From my experience, you can hear the same thing fifty times from fifty different people, and sometimes it's not until the fiftieth person tells you that it sinks in and changes your life forever. You see, it's not always just the words or the right time; it's the right *messenger*. It's the right tool, the right channel and it's the right time. That's why I call this book, "Time Is Running Out," because life is so precious. We must follow our inner desires and avoid finding excuses, blaming others, and living in fear. I think that 95% of our fears are illusions and once you face them, the thought will disappear.

Recently, I shared, "Don't blame it! Claim it!" with one of my closest friends and students Ju-Lynda. She had come up to me crying that I hurt her feelings when I said something, and although she told herself that I didn't intentionally hurt her, she couldn't resist but to feel hurt. So I explained to always repeat "You hurt my feelings." "I hurt my feelings." When you blame someone else for something, you give your power away to them. When you claim your feelings to yourself, you claim all of your life force energy back to yourself. You can cleanse the negative feelings in your own energy field and transmute them for yourself. It is up to you to keep yourself healthy and strong while building confidence and trust in yourself. It is really hard to not take things personal that others say, and yet it is also hard to always sound nice as to not hurt others feelings. All we can do is our best, and when our best isn't good enough, then encourage yourself and others to work through the experience together.

Because we are all a part of each other, we are all healers and teachers for ourselves and others. No one can really change you, but you. We each have to do our own work, even if we have the greatest teacher in the world guiding us. I believe that we each have different parts to play in this lifetime, just like our bodies have millions of different parts to play inside our own physical body. We are so amazing, and have so much potential; it's time to recognize that and honor ourselves and this beautiful creation called earth. So, what are you waiting for! Let's grow together!

Ever since I was a child, I wanted to be an elder. I wanted to grow old, or so I thought. When I turned thirty, I finally realized that I didn't want to be old. I just wanted to be wise, so that I could share the love and wisdom with others. I knew that I would never stop growing, and when I did, I wouldn't be living anymore. So I decided that I would always live. I learned that when you are growing for your highest good, life is not always simple and easy. If you want an easy road, then you want a road that doesn't involve growth and understanding. I have often found that right before another spiritual growth period I go through a very trying time or a time of boredom where the energy is clearing. What gets me through those moments is to recognize that I am growing and to keep giving gratitude for all of my lessons and teachers.

I can tell when I am going through a period of growth by all of the changes, or the amount of hardships that I encounter in a short period of time. I also know that I tend to run away from my problems, which will stunt my growth, so I am learning to stop running and face them so that I can keep growing. For example, if you are in a relationship that does not meet your needs or is causing you pain and stress, then you might decide to walk away. However, then you will start a new relationship with a different person, and the same situation occurs with them. Now, this time, you chose to take blame for the situation and get to the root of the problem to resolve it. Perhaps something you may have done long time ago that you have not forgiven yourself for, so you are putting yourself in the other person's shoes to receive the pain that you may have given long time ago. However, oftentimes, we just get stuck in the same pattern until we teach ourselves to stand up for ourselves and face it.

In order to continue to grow, you must take time contemplating, accepting who you are and your own actions. You must become responsible for your words and actions and be willing to take a stand for yourself and what you want out of life. Trusting your abilities to be able to change and go for after what you want in life takes a lot of patients, confidence and trust in the universe. There are many different ways to assist each person in their growth, as we all learn in different ways. You many have already heard or understand how powerful journaling and reciting your intentions out-loud may be. Writing your intentions for your future is one of the most important things to concentrate your time on. Your thoughts, words, and actions all play a part in your present moment as well as your future.

You can be as detailed as you want when concentrating on what you need in your life in order to focus in on your goals. Just make sure that you focus on your end result and leave room for the unknown, because a lot of times we do not know what the universe has in store for us to assist us, but can recognize it when it happens. Therefore, one of you affirmations that you write may be, "I will recognize when the universe creates a new doorway to help me on my path."

Know that you are able to inspire and support yourself when needed.

Write at least five to ten affirmations in your journal that you can reference too when you are in need of inspiration.

_____

_____

_____

Here are Some Affirmations and Reminders I Recite for Myself:

"Today I will grow towards my fullest potential."

"Today I may be tired, but I know this rest will rejuvenate me for a larger task at hand."

"I understand that life has challenges and through challenges comes great realizations."

"I am grateful for all of my experiences because they will bring forth beauty in my future."

"I am happy to nurture myself with water, fresh air, and live food, because I deserve to grow healthy."

"Each day I grow stronger with wisdom from experiences meeting new people and traveling to different places."

"Today I am thankful for the earth, the water, the fire, and the air for keeping me in balance with my destiny."

"Each day, I remain grateful for being on my path and reaching all of my goals."

After you have written down some affirmations for yourself, make sure that you have acknowledged all of your achievements as well. This may be the opposite for some people. They may have achieved so much in their life, that they have not taken the time to just enjoy your life, and this may be where there needs to be growth. Self-love is a huge part of growing. It seems that taking care of our needs is one of the most difficult things to do on earth. Make sure, that you grow from the inside out and not just all around you. Just like beauty, true growth starts from within.

CHAPTER EIGHT

₪ Heal the Mind to Heal the Body

"You must first heal the mind in order to heal the physical body."

~Crystal D. Gingras~

The way I understand the process of the human system as a whole is you won't go running unless your mind tells you to go run; you won't go drinking unless your mind tells you to go get a drink; you will not begin to eat healthier if your mind does not direct you to do so. It is difficult to acquire inner peace without practicing silence, because silence is what quiets the mind. For years my mind would rant and babble all night long, not allowing me any rest. The mind would replay the day, the year, and, on occasion, my complete life story. Every so often, my mind would keep me stirring for days without rest.

I realized that my disoriented mind was the one who kept me trapped in these consistent patterns night after night, year after year. My mind was the one troubled by the dark, fearful to get robbed or raped. I heard every minute sound outside or inside and lay there frozen in terror. I used to sleep with a knife in my hand wondering if that was the doorknob that I heard downstairs from my bedroom loft. I would look out of the windows and make sure that all of my doors were locked. I know that these are all extreme cases of the mind being trapped in an emotion that needs to be released, but sometimes we are just thinking about bills and kids and what to make for dinner. An experience is an experience, no matter what, they are each valid and each our own.

When I started teaching Reiki classes after the year 2000, I found out that in Japan they practiced a technique of Reiki of holding the hands together (Gassho) in silence in front of the heart while concentrating on the two middle fingers. When the mind wanders off into all of your thoughts again, then go back to focusing on the middle fingers again. The importance of silence is to stop and gather your energy and concentrate on yourself, silence, and balancing your own energy before you even begin to help someone else balance their body. When you are a Reiki practitioner, you practice Gassho at least

20 minutes a day and it's good to practice right before you give a Reiki treatment. It is very important to have the mind clear before working on another person in order to be clear.

There are people who have spent more than half of their lifetimes diagnosing people who have physical disorders by diagnosing the mind. In fact, many people who practice natural healing or shamanic healing (there are many names for people who love to help others), use the practice of having the person name their pain by naming a person, place, thing or oftentimes a color. It's actually a very simple process that just takes practice to gain confidence like anything else. Also, there are many people who have studied where the emotions are stored in the body.

Over the past ten years of doing massages and energy work on people, I found that attachments to diseased relatives or loved ones have caused a lot of hip pain. I started asking each of my clients who came to mind when I would put pressure on the hip pain. One person responded that they lost a younger brother when they were child, and one person had lost a spouse. You can ask yourself who the first person is that comes to mind that might have died in the family when the pain started. Then, work on releasing the attachment in the mind that is causing the pain. The attachment may be caused because you need to grieve over that person more, or there needs to be forgiveness.

I have also noticed that the pain on the left side of the body where energy flows in is feminine energy, so any attachment with a woman in your life that has not be released or forgiven may cause pain and suffering in this area (male energy on the right side, where energy flows out). Some people may keep injuring certain places on their body because they have not forgiven themselves for causing harm to someone, so they are acting out their shame or guilt in the physical world. Sometimes the wound may have been buried twenty or thirty years ago without allowing the self any time to grieve.

Another finding is that if you are a person who works on others and are also studying what mental pain causes physical suffering in your client's body, you will more than likely get more patients or clients with the same mental/physical problems. I believe this is the manifestation of working on a particular area or block so that when you learn how to clear that energy, it is attracted towards you for healing when those persons are honestly looking for help.

I began my journey of self healing in 2007. I decided that I wanted to devote a year to focus on myself and healing. Once I made this decision to take time off, my business slowed down, and I ended up closing my office that I had for three years. It was painful for me as I had an attachment to my office and the healing space where I had spent many hours of my life, sometimes even sleeping there. I was working on many people each day and also had three other massage therapists, and energy workers with me there. I had devoted all of my time there to help other people, which limited my time with my friends and family, and most importantly, with myself. In November of 2007, I decided to take a trip to Guatemala. I ended a three-year relationship and moved out my personal belongings two days before I left to Guatemala. I had made up my mind to take care of myself fully and release all of the things in my life that were no longer serving my highest good.

I arrived in Guatemala in about twenty-two hours with no sleep. I was very tired and hungry. I was joining a class there to do a trance dance facilitators' training class, and before I left, I still did not know who was going to pick me up from the airport, or what time. On the plane, I spoke for several hours with a man on the plane there for several hours that produced films on medicine people in the area, and he warned me to be careful of thieves and danger. He offered me a ride to his place to figure things out, but I thought I would stay and figure things out on my own.

Since I was starving and cold, I was so delighted to see an old woman with a metal box coming down the way, which had hand-made tamales and bread. I paid her one U.S. dollar, and in return I received a cup of coffee, tamale, and one piece of bread. I cried as the coffee warmed my throat and soul, and the bread and tamale warmed my stomach. There was a pitiful dog whimpering about, so I shared my food with him as tears flooded down my face.

After I finished and dried my tired tears, I walked closely around the front of the airport which was being remodeled and had plastic up everywhere. Hundreds of people started to come outside, and there were hundreds of relatives and friends waiting to pick them up. Hours passed by and the sun finally began to rise over the sky, and I sat down on a cement wall nearby with my luggage held close in hand. A kind woman stopped by and asked if I was ok, and I asked to borrow a telephone to call a contact number I had saved. There was no answer, so shortly after I took out my notebook and drew a sign with the name of the group that I was meeting in hopes someone would find me.

About three more hours passed and it was nearly noon when two women came up to me and said they had just flown in from Belize for the same workshop. They said we still had a few hours, so we walked to a nearby market by the zoo there and had some snacks and looked around. The colors were so amazing, and the faces of the market people were filled with welcome smiles. These beautiful women were my angels, and I finally felt at peace. The time flew by, and we walked back to the airport to meet with more people arriving. Then we took the bus to another city about three hours away and caught a boat ride across Lake Atitlan where we stayed at beautiful Villa Sumaya.

The sun was setting as we took the boat over, and I was sure I was in heaven. I shared a room there with one of my angels from the airport and fell into a deep, peaceful sleep. I awoke very early in the morning and walked about looking at all the green, lush trees and plants, and as I watched the huge, brilliant sunrise, healing tears flowed down my checks. I was very humbled as I felt the pain release from my head. Even the arthritic feelings in my wrists and fingers from years of hard work and car accidents pulled away from my physical body. This place was magical and so powerful. The headaches and stomach pains I had suffered for years were no longer there.

I would like to share more of what my incredible experiences were like in Guatemala, and I think the best way is to recite word for word from my personal journal. November 11, 2007. "Woke up at 3:30 a.m. with a dream of flying off the highway with my sister Eva, then I laid back down for two more hours. The birds called me in the morning to wake me up, and then I did a prayer for clarity. I braided my long hair and thanked the Creator for all my blessings and new friends. I already knew that I needed to learn to just be; to live in the moment and not dwell on the past or the future." Note: "I love how the boats drop off the workers in the mornings."

"We took a boat to Chi Chi (Guatemala market chichicastenango) today. They have the most colorful clothing and jewelry. I bought a jade and rose quarts bracelet and then I spent the rest of my money in the Shaman area with all of the natural medicine. They had copal, candles, and some small round charcoal bundles with about fifteen pieces of mixed up medicine."

I went to the church where a man told me about St. Michael Archangel. Notably, we have a Michael on the trip that is named after him. (Nicole and Michael). "There was this Mayan man in the temple that asked me if I wanted some explanation about the old church, and I thought he was another tour guide trying to make money. However, he told me about the beautiful wooden piece on the wall and then told me that I needed to go to this older church a few blocks away. He had felt something in my spirit that I cannot explain with words, and knew that I needed to go. I had already gone to this church a few days before and so I asked him what was in the room to the right. When I had arrived to the smaller church a few days prior to meeting this man, I was very drawn to this room to the right which had an empty glass case with blankets. I was drawn to light a candle and offer sacred tobacco at the door. I felt that there was a High Priestess or Priest who was buried there, and the man verified that it was the preceding Priest."

"After the group that I went to Guatemala with left the church, we walked up a mountain to an ancient Mayan church." This church did not have walls, or separated sides for Mayans and Catholics, this church was outside." There was a shaman holding burning copal in a can to clear the people that came with the smoke (see the picture on the back cover of me praying on the mountain with him in the background) The Shamans do the same procedure at the big church in the chichicastenango market place. There was a huge fire and rocks on top of the mountain where you go and pray that I believe stays lit every day." While we were up there praying, we did the Hu chant together. Hu is an ancient sound for healing."

"After we came back down from the church, I got some fresh tacos from the market place. These were delicious Guatemalan tacos with corn tortillas, chicken, pico de gallo, grilled onions, pineapple, and lettuce. I also ventured to the shamans block in the market place and purchased some copal and charcoal with mixed healing herbs and tobacco for ceremonies (I still have charcoals five years later)." After we got back to Villa Sumaya, I decided to jump in Lake Atitlan hungrily waiting for dinner. The lake was so refreshing and beautiful that I shouted out a loud trill (loud, high-pitched vibration sound made with the tongue moving up and down very fast)." From this resource, this rich land with culture, aliveness in the earth, trees, water and all surroundings, I was able to start my healing.

This was my first experience of how powerful the mind absolutely is and how I came to the conclusion of where the healing has to begin. I had decided that I was coming here to begin my year of self-healing and because I followed through with taking this trip, I was able to begin my cleansing. It is now a little over three years since then, and I am still on my journey of self-healing. A huge part of my healing and cleansing is completing this book. I understand that completing something is very important if you have made up your mind to finish it. I also believe that you can change your mind at anytime and decide not to finish something, but finishing it, if you have made up your mind to do so, and brings a peace and confidence in your decision.

Making up your mind to trust that you are always being guided and protected by whatever it is that you call your divine is important. As I said earlier, the divine to me is Love or God. And, as many say, God is Love and nothing else. I know that love was surrounding me the day I left the Guatemala airport. The night before I had missed my flight when the group I was with arrived to the airport for departures.

One new friend from our group, Faith, gave me fifty dollars which covered my hostel for the evening and part of the flight change the next day. My other friend Michael gave me several dollars that he had left in his wallet before his flight took off after he found out I was stranded. After I paid for my flight the next afternoon and checked my luggage, I started to walk back to go through customs to board my plane. I was not aware that I had to buy a visa to get back to the United States. So, when I arrived at the window and they said $1 for my visa, I looked in my wallet, and all I had was a single dollar bill. I handed him the dollar bill, received my visa and tears flowed down my face as I walked down the hall. Sometimes one dollar means more than you could ever possibly imagine.

Here is the story as it's written in my journal that day. "Well, I'm here at Gate 12. It's 11:45 a.m. I board at 1 p.m. I was crying for about twenty minutes because I was so blessed. When Michael and Nicole left, he gave me his last 7 dollars, and I accepted. I had 12 dollars in my wallet, plus the 50 I found and the 50 Faith had given to me. When I got my ticket it was 112 which left me with 3 left over for the taxes. I was praying to Warm Blood Woman and all my Guides and I had been standing by a lot of Missionaries on their way home. If it was 150 like they told me on the phone I would have been short by 38 dollars. Wow. I am so humbled yet again. It is so amazing how they (my guides and ancestors) can help me. I just reminded myself how they said, ask and you shall always receive. Not one dollar to my name and if that's not proof I'm being watched over, then I don't know what is."

The mind is a powerful tool and we all have been given this tool for free. Your mind is something that is yours, and you will need to take time to get to know it every day. Our minds are very alike, yet very different. We are each very unique because the mind is so unlimited, and one lifetime is not enough to see and explore all the possibilities of the mind. It is up to you to decide how you would like to use this tool and apply it. It helps you to learn and explore beautiful and new things daily.

If you are smiling now, reading this book out loud, receiving new ideas as you read, or even inventing new possibilities and understanding, then you are using your mind. Maybe you are now planning a trip to Guatemala or a place that you have always dreamed about. The mind is always at work; it is up to us to learn how to listen, understand, and utilize this tool for our best and highest good. Yes, indeed, my relatives the mind is the most powerful and accessible tool!

CHAPTER NINE

₪ The Four Directions

*"Great Spirit; Creator; Tirawa; This One: Crystal D.
Gingras, Chapette Hetas, Calls on Your Guidance and Support at
This Time. I Call on the Powers and the Spirits of the East ... the
South ... the West ... the North ...the All the Directions In-
between, to Come and Hear My Prayer. I Pray to Father Sky and to
Mother Earth. I Thank You; I Appreciate You; I Honor You; I
Love You."*

~Crystal D. Gingras~

Breathing in the sacred breath of life as I
awake, I give thanks for my life again on
earth. I drink a glass of water and give thanks to the water for my
body, mind, and spirit. I take some tobacco outside to offer my

thanks and gratitude to the four directions and the directions in between. I start with the direction east for the new day and new beginnings. After I say all of my prayers out loud to the East, I then ask for the gifts and energies of the East to fill my being with all of their powers and offer a pinch of tobacco. Then, I move to the South and go around to the West and then the North. The directions in-between are the Southeast, Southwest, Northwest, and Northeast.

Some of the meanings vary from country to country and culture, but ultimately we were (are) all one, and we all share the same four directions on earth. In the morning, I have learned to offer tobacco to greet the sun and give thanks for our life because without the sun, we would not have life on this planet. In the evening, I learned to offer blue corn or cornmeal to the moon, because the corn represents food, nourishment, and the cycle of life from seed to sustenance. You can also offer water to show your gratitude to the new day, or as you call in the powers and spirits of the directions to honor all of them with gratitude at the end of the day.

The direction East, I think of as the color yellow because the sun rises for each new day. I also think of the East as the direction of the Eagle with new clean energy and new beginnings. I think of this direction as the element of air because of the strength of the new energy that it always brings forth. I call upon the direction of the East when I am lost or confused and need a new beginning. I call on this direction when I feel unsafe and need protection. This direction also brings me powerful energy when I am feeling weak, because the sun is the strength of all people of this land.

The direction South is the color red and the direction of the Red Road. I was taught that the Red Road means that you are following your truth path or spiritual path by living and seeing through love and trust. I think of this direction as the element of the earth because it is red like the earth and the mountains and my people. I call on the bear in the south for strength to love myself and all others just as they are in this moment. The bear is also the healing of my Pawnee people, who help to keep us strong and warm, and who give healing power to our people. The chiefs and elders of our nation wore bear claws around their necks to represent their strength and their medicine.

The direction west is the color black and represents the night, the deep dark waters of looking within and the beautiful Shell Woman of the waters. I think of this direction as the element of the water because it represents the deepest parts of the oceans where it is pitch black. The West is where you decide to take that journey down to the darkness where your fears are hidden or things that you do not want to face. They may be buried thousands of feet down where no human and most water animals cannot even travel. This direction helps you to face your past or things that you are not aware of that are holding you back. This is a place of owning your power and becoming whole.

The direction north represents ancient wisdom, knowledge, cold winters, changes, and sometimes difficult life lessons. I think of this direction as the element of fire because it is powerful and comes with great responsibility. This is a place of purity, where fire can burn away everything that is no longer needed in your life. Call on this direction to clear away the remains of the past to be ready when you call on the direction of the East again to start new. When you carry wisdom from the north, you are being asked to share, protect and help to guide the people the best that you can.

There are also the four winds that many people have prayed to for many years to call on the energies of a particular direction. The winds help to make all of the changes and may seem difficult at first while you are whirling through the changes that need to be made in order to grow through experiences. The winds are powerful, and they help stir up all of the elements in order to put them back in balance again. This reminds me of defragmenting a computer to realign all of the unused space that has been used and then deleted and then becomes permanently removed, only to be changed once again.

Last night on my laptop, I was watching a beautiful movie where the woman blows the conch shell to the four winds to ask permission before they begin to dance on the grapes for harvest day. The movie was about a family-owned vineyard which ended up being consumed by fire. The owner of the vineyard, the father, was icy and solemn throughout the entire movie. When the fire came, he cried, and his heart opened up, reconnecting him with his family again. There was one last grape vine that was saved by the son, and he was able to start new again. Another movie that I watched a man lost all of his crops and he felt like his entire livelihood was destroyed, then three days later, his crops came back to life.

The conch shell is popularly used in many cultures to call upon the ancestors of the four directions, the wind, and the water. The shell is a symbol of the water and also of the wind as it plays music as a wind instrument. Certain tribes and cultures may be closely connected to a particular direction because of their location for growing and harvesting food and crops. Tribes of people also have different animals, plants, and spirits that they pray and use as symbols for their flags and shields because they are what help feed and clothe all the people.

If you were to research more about the four directions, you will find many different animals and different colors to represent each one. Symbols and colors are extremely powerful and do more than characterize and represent something. They help to call on our ancestors and helper spirits whom are often relatives of the tribe, community, or family. The way that families honor their ancestors and celebrate harvest will remain the same because their relatives will usually reincarnate within their own family or tribe.

For example, the grandmother who passed away will now be reborn as the granddaughter or grandson. Some cultures believe that spirits do not reincarnate, but only take on the karma of the relative that passed away, making them seem familiar. A nurse I spoke with that was watching me do healing work on my nephew who had cancer said that she lost a brother when she was little and that he reincarnated to be her son. She said that she believed in reincarnation because he looked exactly like her brother. This also happened with someone else that I know whose daughter lost a young child. Years later, he was reborn again and grew to look and act exactly the same. She had pictures of both of them and shared with me their remarkable resemblance. I believe that if I have heard a couple stories like this, then there are many more of the same out there.

There are people who will pray to one direction or face a certain direction for certain things. For example, you can face the north when experiencing hard times to ask for the wisdom from your lessons for growth. Or, you may face the south when looking for or following your truth path and listen to the heart, and work with love. The directions in-between are just as powerful by honoring the Southeast, Southwest, Northwest, and the Northeast. These are called the cardinal directions, and there are many indigenous peoples who pray to these directions each day for their strength and medicine. I have experienced strong spirit helpers that are always sitting in those directions.

One day there was a woman who wanted to do a sweat lodge ceremony with me, so I felt honored to share that sacred space with her. The time that we spent together was blessed by a deer when we were making our prayer ties with tobacco. We heard the deer walking around in the direction of the North, and then it walked around the east and then walked up to us through the South. The deer only stayed for a short time, but came near inside of the sacred circle as if offering greetings of gratitude and healing for the ceremony.

After the fire was ready and the energy was cleansed and balanced inside the lodge with white sage, I felt an elder spirit man sitting in the Northwest of the lodge. She said that was where her grandfather always sat for ceremony. This was an additional confirmation for her that this was a wholesome time and lodge for her to participate in ceremony. I was honored and humbled that day by the deer nation and her ancestors.

You also honor the Great Spirit, or Father Sky above, and the Mother Earth. It is good to face and raise your hands up to each direction, and then place your hands on Mother Earth and connect with her vibrations. This will also help you to ground and connect to the higher realms and all of creation each day. It always feels good to give thanks to all of the ancestors of the land, the trees and plants of the land, and so on. Whatever comes to your mind, or what you see before you, give thanks to while in prayer. If you do not have a particular prayer, than giving thanks is the prayer. You will notice a lot of changes in your life right away when giving gratitude.

Giving thanks and gratitude to the sky, earth, and waters was a daily routine long ago that was lost by many years of change and experiences. I believe that it is important for us to start giving our thanks once again to help balance out the cycles of life and the seasons. To give your gratitude is to show appreciation and love for all of life and when you do that, you support life on earth. There are not enough words, pictures, songs, or sentences to explain the depth of the importance of offering gratitude to the four-directions and the elements and all that is represented in each direction. There is such a great need for gratitude right now that if you only have enough strength to just pray and offer gratitude for just Mother Earth, or just the water, then please do so. If something in particular calls to your heart or resonates within you, then give thanks for that one thing, just once, each and every day.

Here is an example about symbols working with you on earth. I had a massage client who was a real estate agent. He had a bad rotator cuff. It was on his left side, so I knew it was feminine energy. It was something to do with his mother, grandmother, or great-grandmother and so on for seven generations. I was explaining this to him, and he said honestly that he did not believe in past lives or reincarnation. I explained this is how to release this frozen pain you have inside.

I began to see symbols on his back, and then I saw two rows of men in armor standing above him with a distinct symbol on their shields. The symbol was blue and yellow, and I explained this to him and said they were his ancestors and they are here to help you heal. Even though he told me he disbelieved in how I was working I kept explaining to him exactly what I was doing and what I could see in other dimensions as I worked on him. The symbols were glowing on and around his shoulder and I traced them with my finger one by one until they disappeared. After his appointment, he was smiling and swinging his arm around and he pulled his business card out of his wallet, and on it was a picture of him with a huge smile, a beard and Kings jeweled crown and staff with the blue and yellow symbol I had explained to him. He looked me in the eyes and said, "Now I believe."

The four directions are the pathways to our ancestors, helpers, guides, animal helpers. It is up to us to ask for their help, even if you are simply giving thanks to them each day. A prayer is like a thought. It is up to you to have good thoughts and utilize the beautiful gift of gratitude, compassion, and love that we all carry within.

CHAPTER TEN

₪ Plants, Herbs & Vines as Medicine

"Honor the healer for his services, for the Lord created him. His skill comes from the Most High, and he is rewarded by kings. The healer's knowledge gives him high standing and wins him the admiration of the great. The Lord has created medicines from the earth, and a sensible man will not disparage them."

~Apocrypha, Ecclesiasticus, Chapter 38~

"Thank you so much plants, herbs and vines for providing healing for so many people for so many years. Thank you for the healing that you have given me and the knowledge that you continue to share with me. I will do my best to honor each of you in the best way that I can at this time."

~Crystal D. Gingras~

For this chapter, I have to give an extra special thanks and gratitude to the plant nation because they are so important for our every day mental, physical, and spiritual well-being and balance. They are our foods, our medicine when we eat, and our beauty that we look at all around us. They are the way of life for many healers who give their natural medicine to thousands of sick people all over the world every day in form of roots, leaves, powder, teas, and oils.

As early as I can remember, my mother was providing our family with natural medicine which includes many plants and herbs. Through my lifetime, we had an aloe vera plant in the house for cuts and burns. I remember burning my hands while cooking numerous times, and there was always a plant available to sooth my pain. When ingesting internally, it is great for clearing out the small and large intestines and very popular in flavored drinks.

I also remember seeing the aloe vera plant around the sacred fire for a healing ceremony. This particular ceremony was a part of a workshop that lasted seven days. This was my first time that I had ever met a Mayan-Aztec and Toltec teacher, and we used the aloe vera plant as a part of the medicine. We took several pieces to spread around the outside of the fire. I also ask the plant for help and place it in my sacred space when someone is in need of healing. Plants do not always have to be applied topically or ingested; they can also be in the room and asked for their help, similar to asking a tree for help.

My mother had natural pills for almost everything, including headaches and insomnia. I loved seeing my mother in her clay masks around her face with her beautiful smile and eyes shining though the clay as it dried. She made teas and burned sage, cedar, and sweet grass. I always loved the smell of the plant medicines burning in an abalone shell or small cast iron skillet. The sage would be either white sage from California or local sage that we would go pick and bundle together. We used different colored cotton strings and placed the sage together in bundles while it was still fresh and then let it dry to burn later.

The sage is then used to clear away any positive ions that are in the energy field or home and bring in negative ions that are good for you. Often, we would use a fan from a winged-one, such as an eagle or a hawk for clearing. The hawk fans have a very gentle clearing effect, and the eagle feathers have a very strong effect. The smell has been one of my favorite smells and oftentimes is my perfume mixed with sweet grass!

The energy is cleared in your home and around your energy body with these medicines. I often use them every day, and they are present in almost every ceremony that I have attended. Some families will only use the cedar, but it is flat cedar, and it is burned for healing, prayers, and for clearing any negative energy for the person and for the home. Sage is very popular as a tea and insect repellent and is plentiful in different places of the world. I remember watching a film of survival in Africa and they rubbed the sage all over to help with insects and animals. They said that it helps to keep the mosquitoes away as well as hiding their scent from predators. Sage is also applied for cuts or burns to heal the skin. One of my favorite sages is the California white sage, and the other is the sage I get from South Dakota. I have also noticed at ceremonies that the white sage is liked by many elders for cleansing negative energies.

Recently, I have studied the South American plants and vines. They are available for healing and clearing for the body, mind, and home and are very powerful and sacred. As we begin to open our minds and let the ego and judgment fall away, we are beginning to share our ways of healing with different countries and to understand that we need to forgive and come together as one again so Mother Earth can heal herself. We are all in this together, and if we work together as one family sharing our medicine and our ways with those that are willing to participate, we can forgive and accept these changes at a much faster rate to benefit everyone on Mother Earth. I understand that these ways might go against some of our old belief systems from the past, but as the earth spins, it changes, and it's time for us to adapt and see the good in ourselves and in each other.

We now have the gift of the internet where we can find

almost any answer that we are looking for, and it's so easy to locate a library or a computer for most of us. For those in different countries, it is up to the leaders to travel and meet with the elders, leaders, medicine people, and chiefs of the different nations and tribes to start working together and understanding the different medicines that we have available. Many of the trees that I will mention in this book are only a very few species of what is available to us all over the world. Many of the plants and medicines are available to be grown. It is the lack of knowledge and application that we are experiencing at this moment.

Natural farming and permaculture are starting to come back into place once again. Permaculture is a natural way of growing plants, corn, and food without adding chemicals and unnatural substances. State by state here on Turtle Island they are learning to implement new plans to be more environmental and energy friendly and to plant trees and plants per so many square feet in the cities. Code standards are being revised by people and companies who are realizing the importance of becoming "green." Smaller communities are realizing how important it is to start making a change within their own neighborhoods and communities and learning about all the plants that are essential to overall health.

Learning to honor and respect the plant people, just as we need to respect and honor the water, the sky, and Mother Earth, is essential. The plant nation is a part of many of our natural and western medicines. Plants are in many hair products and skin care all over the world, and we would not be here without their help. I worked with a company for awhile that used many different plants such as: sage, coneflower, burdock root, aloe barbadensis, and chamomile. Some places in the world still use certain plants for hair and skin care without other added ingredients. There are many natural medicines, as well as western medicine that are mixed with other western medicine to heal specific ailments. We, in fact, need all of them to survive.

I would like to share as much as I can in this book, but I encourage those of you who feel called to do so, please look up more information and get involved in your own community. Where I am living now in Dallas, I notice that there are many people here who grow their own herbs and gardens and many stores carry lots of natural herbs and body care with plants, flowers and roots. It's time to make a change, starting with you and your community.

A very popular plant that I have noticed in Texas is rosemary. There are huge plants in the back of the massage school that I attended in Plano and a lot of residential homes have rosemary plants in their front yards. Rosemary is very good for healing, protection, and calming. It is a great plant for relaxing the mind and the body. When I was at a ceremony in San Jose California, I placed rosemary in the four directions for the women's moon lodge teepee. We had a lot of plant medicine in there for the women on their moon time (menstrual period). Some of the plants were whole plants like the rosemary that I hung on the inside of the teepee, and some plants were extracted into essential oils that people could spray on or apply from a bottle.

What makes some plants very important is that they can protect gardens and crops from insects and animals. For example, lemon balm will assist in protecting your garden from insects. Also, sunflowers are great because their long green leaves are similar to the praying mantis, and insects are afraid to get eaten! Planting certain plants or flowers is like placing an eagle or an owl statue to keep the small birds away. All plants and vines have specific roles to play on earth just as each of us. Some of them can provide grounding and centering, and some may provide healing and protection. Now days, you only hear about the physical assistance that they offer us by drinking them in tea, but you do not hear very much about their mental and spiritual properties. This usually takes more research and learning from an experienced teacher, or spending time with the plant itself.

Again, this may sound funny or something out of this world, but if you take the time and perseverance, then you can ask the plant yourself what all of its properties are. I recommend finding someone that works with plants and have them assist you in your learning process. Some people are born with the gift to hear plants and what they can do, and many people are taught from their parents or grandparents. A good way to begin this process if you are interested is to start eating healthy and work on becoming clear and open to receiving.

There is also a ceremony in South America that is called Ayahuasca ceremony. These ceremonies are now practiced in many different places by drinking a tea made by someone who has studied the plants and vines in areas like Peru and Brazil. Whenever someone prepares medicine from the trees and plants, they always ask permission and give thanks for their help. If someone was sick in their stomach and they just needed one particular plant, then they will let the plant know that their sister is sick and needs healing. Then they will extract the plant and give an offering for its help. An offering may be anything from the heart that has meaning from the person collecting the plant, or from the person sick who needs the medicine.

Another important aspect to share about plants and nature is that they all need respect and appreciation. For example, today I prepared the land here on my reservation to start our community garden. First, I took some water and offered some to the four directions, then to father sky and mother earth. Then I sang a song to offer the spirits and ancestors of the land appreciation and gratitude. After I did that, I took some time to talk with all of the insects, birds, and animals that are on the land and even under the land. I asked them if they would please move around the fenced area of where the garden will be. I let everyone and everything know that we will be digging up the earth to plant a garden, and that this garden will grow food to feed the people. I also thought that we could grow some food and seeds behind the fence in the wild for the animals, and that will be just for them.

This is the old way and is very important to start doing again. The insects and birds know how to work the land together and sing for rain to take care of the land. Every day the ants and insects are working and the birds are watching and talking. I share this with you in hopes that if you are growing a garden or know someone who is, especially in a new area, they can help by doing something similar or finding someone who can come do this for them. This is how I bless the land and create a place of peace and good harmony.

The plant people, rock people, and tree people all appreciate people who let them know what they are doing. A lot of people collect rocks from their travels and forget to ask or tell the rock why they are taking them. Stone people are very sacred to many people and have been around for many years for healing and wisdom. In almost every culture there are different uses and medicines for many of the natural kingdom. If you choose to practice any healings or ceremonies, I recommend doing your own research and self-meditation to connect with all people and plants that will be included.

CHAPTER ELEVEN

₪ Trees as Medicine

"Great Spirit of this tree, please hear my heart and guide me in the right direction. Please assist me with your strength and energy to release the fear that I no longer need and all other blocks that no longer serve me. Help me to accept the things in life that I need to survive in a balanced and loving way. Thank you for supporting me and all of life. Thank you; thank you; thank you. I love you; I love you; I love you."

~Crystal D. Gingras~

When I was in elementary school I would have dreams about bathing the elderly and giving them a place to sleep. I would look at

all of the electrical poles and lines going through the tall trees. I noticed all the tops of the trees

being cut in awkward positions to go around all of the wires. Anger and sadness would fill my heart and pour down my face. I always wondered why and who could do such a thing to our Grandfather trees? It took many years to transform this heart full of anger and sadness into love and motivation to help the children of the earth today. I thought if there was a movie, "alien versus trees," it would be all of the huge transformers outside that come to life and battle against all of the tall tree poles that have been cut into electrical conduits for electricity.

The tree nation is a strong and vast nation that spreads out all over the world. I do know that the original people of this land, Turtle Island, that is now known as America, still has over a million different nations. I was not aware that there was still this many different nations until I supervised for the Census Bureau in 1999-2000 in Topeka. Trees are one of the ancient one's who have lived longer than the two-leggeds have walked on this earth. Besides being a tree hugger all of my life, my interest in trees started around the year 2006 when I spoke to a man who did his healing initiation with a 2,000 year old Yew tree in Scotland. He shared with me some of his experiences with cleansing out the old energies that caused sickness and pain in his physical body. I knew that westerners used knowledge from medicine people in other countries for inflammation and pain medicine, but I was not aware that people still worked with trees for years on a personal level. I was so grateful to know that just one person spent so many years connecting with a tree for healing.

In the indigenous cultures, we honor the trees and ask for their guidance, healing, wisdom, strength, and almost anything that we need. Trees are utilized for many different tools and parts of sacred tools in ceremonies and healing. Almost all handles and staffs are made from trees and then the medicine of the winged ones and four-leggeds were attached. Each tribe used a different way to make their staffs for their people depending on what crops they utilized or what type of healing was taking place. Medicine people utilize the bark to make different teas for different ailments. There are a lot of trees that were used for almost any ailment that is in the physical and emotional body. In the chapter on plants and vines, I talk about the Ayahuasca tree, or vine, that is brewed into tea, and made to drink for almost any ailment. It is widely used with the Chakaruna tree which stories tell that those two trees together can work through any ailment when drank as a tea.

The women of my nation, Pawnee, were the ones who built our lodges out of large tree bodies. The poles that we used were very well rounded and stood very tall. Our homes and ceremonial spaces are called mud lodges or well known as earth lodges. There were many other nations besides the Pawnee (Pani) that lived in earth lodges such as the Otoe nation. My aunt Blanche shared many stories with me about the other tribes that were similar to us such as the Arikiras and the Caddos. We all respected their life and understood their protection and guidance. The remaining structures built from the trees that we lived in are preserved in Kearney, Nebraska where tourists and students take trips to see how we lived.

There are certain trees, such as the cedar tree, that help to repel insects, as well as keep our medicine and people safe. Medicine is anything sacred that we held in high regard, such as eagle feathers (and other feathers), sacred pipes or carving tools. Cedar boxes are commonly used to this day for feather and rattle boxes. Cedar trees are also used to make cradle boards for babies; then depending on the nation, families use deer skin, buffalo or elk skin to enclose the baby.

The Pawnee's and many other different tribes will sing to the trees to offer their respect. Each tribe has their own way of doing ceremonies to respect the earth, the trees, the streams and other forms of life while they are traveling. Say, if they are moving their family to a different part of the lands, then they will stop and pay respects to the trees before they pass through by singing them a song. Or, if they needed to all cross a stream in order to reach their destination, they would sing a song to the waters. This way, it lets them know that they mean no harm, and they are only passing through with respect.

Here is the song in Pawnee that is sung to the trees and water to honor them:

"Wi-ra u-haki, wi-ra u-haki

Ka-tu-haru u-haki, wi-ra u-haki

Ka-tu-haru u-haki,

Wi-ra u-haki, Wi-ra u-haki

Ki-cha-haru u-haki, wi-ra u-haki

Ki-cha-haru u-haki

Wi-ra wi-haku, wi-ra wi-haku

Ki-cha-haru wi-haku, wi-ra wi-haku

Ki-cha-haru wi-haku"

(*) The Hako

Another common tree is the eucalyptus tree that helps to heal the lungs and fungal infections and to strengthen bones and nails. Eucalyptus leaves are commonly used for teas, and I also add them to my tobacco mix to smoke in pipe ceremony as well. Also, you can peel some of the bark off to soak in hot water for tea for ailments. There are different kinds of eucalyptus that work better on different fungal infections. For example, yesterday I saw a doctor and he had fungus on his nail and I told him about eucalyptus radiata for clearing nail fungus.

One of my favorite trees that I have been working with for over twenty years is the white willow tree. When I started going to sweat lodge ceremonies as a child, I learned that the trees that make the lodge are willow trees and that they carry strong medicine. I also started using white willow bark powder to alleviate inflammation in the body years ago. To this day, I use white willow bark for upset stomach, teeth, gums, and even small cuts. I ask for help from the tree for the specific ailment that I need help with for myself, or for the person I am helping. It is always important to ask the tree out loud for what you need assistance with, and to only take what you need, and nothing more or less. The trees are happy to help us, and it is important to leave a gift under the tree in exchange for their help. Some people will offer coins, corn, tobacco, or something that is sacred and meaningful to them. People have been giving offering to trees for their help for thousands of years, and this is still practiced today universally.

There are now many different resources out there to research what trees can assist you with, their origin, and what medicines they carry. I always believe the best way is to spend time with them in meditation and see what you feel from them on your own. There is nothing like connecting with them on your own time and learning from the source what they can help you with. Teas are made from the bark and the leaves and of course, almonds, butters, juices and flour are made from the nuts and fruits that the trees bare. Trees provide so much nourishment for us in so many different ways.

One afternoon, as I walked through a beautiful, lush, green forest, I asked an oak tree to help guide me in the right direction.

After I stated my intention out loud to the tree, I then poured some of my water around the roots (about 2 feet around the trunk). If I have some tobacco, I may leave that as an offering for the tree's assistance. Some trees are great at offering direction for us, but if you never ask, then they cannot help you. Besides trees having so many different physical medicinal properties, they have other strengths and purposes as well.

If I have no other offering with me when I am out walking, I will offer my spit, coins, or a piece of my hair. In some cultures, it is common to offer silver coins, or beads under the tree when you ask for assistance. What I have learned from experiences is that you offer something from your heart. And, if what you are asking for is very special and important, than you should gift something very special to you and important. The trees are alive and they can listen, talk, and they do appreciate if you tell them that you are cutting them down, pruning, or even planting them.

I worked a couple of weeks with a friend who owned a landscaping and tree trimming business, and he told me how he could hear the trees talking sometimes, and how they even cried sometimes. He said the first time he heard one crying was a tree stump he saw, and ever since then, he made sure to let them know that he was cutting them down and why. For example, if you are trimming a tree so it will not eventually fall onto the roof of your house, you let them know that you are protecting your home and family. This also works the other way as well. If you have a tree outside of your home, you may offer it something and ask it to watch over your home and family. Trees have a very powerful energy and are rooted deeply into Mother Earth and stand very tall as well to Father Sky. The tree nation carries very powerful medicine and only need to be talked to and cared for more. I think that similar to a person, the more you communicate your needs with them, the more they will assist you.

When you are feeling drained or scatter-brained, or perhaps need a great place to connect to your Divine, or your higher source of power, then you can always ask a tree for help. You don't have to become a tree hugger or name your tree in your front yard, but it's great to learn how to connect with them at some point in your life.

If you are scattered or feel like things in your life are spinning out of control, then you can go to a tree, offer something (water, tobacco, a hug), and then squat down with your back against the tree and ask the tree for grounding now. First of all, being in the squatting position helps you to start grounding your root chakra, or your first energy center at the base of your spine. Then, you can take three to ten deep breaths and imagine connecting with the tree and releasing anything that you no longer need in your life through the roots of the tree. You may see the energy being released as sludge, blackness, or a white light flowing through the roots of the tree and deep into the center of Mother Earth. Always remember, when you are done connecting and releasing with the tree, to say thank you and then disconnect from the tree's energy.

When you connect with a tree, your energies become one and depending on the medicine of the tree and what you ask for help, you will feel the different vibration levels of the tree's energy. I suggest trying the grounding meditation with different types of trees and see which one works best for you. Also, when releasing old energies, grounding, or clearing any blocks that you have in the body, you can always use the grounding technique described above. In order to increase the power of release, do this practice during a full moon.

I was very grateful when I moved into my first apartment in Dallas, TX in 2011 because I had the only three pine trees in the area right in front of my patio. Pine trees are great for healing a person's body when made into a tea with the bark. Many people used the sap for a sweetener as well. Pinecones are also very sacred to many different tribes and ancestors. I used the pine needles that fell onto my patio as a part of my smudge with sage and cedar to cleanse my home. They also made excellent kindle for sacred fire for ceremonies and prayers.

There is also a wonderful place in Addison that I go to and ground with the trees. Although there are wires and electrical boxes to light up the small park surrounded by apartments and generators, the trees are still alive. There is a huge grandfather tree with a lot of other very tall slender trees that make for a very relaxing and inviting park. It is now mostly used for dogs to go to the restroom, but in the middle is a waterfall with tables and chairs.

I arrived one day with one of my friends Pat and there was a man there playing the guitar with a very sad melody. After we walked around for a few minutes I said hello to the man and we began a conversation. He was asking what Pat and I did and I told him about Reiki healing. I was explaining how Reiki is Japanese for universal life force energy and that it brings back life and vitality into the body and energy field. He still seemed confused about the whole idea, so I offered a hands-on example of Reiki and he accepted.

I placed my hands on his shoulders and started to call on Reiki and all the Reiki Masters and helpers to come through and work on this relative. In just a few minutes there was heat flowing through to him and as I took a deep breath and prepared to breath out and remove my hands. I opened my eyes, and saw the energy from all of the trees beaming a stream of light towards him and then as my hands removed from his body, this darkness from his chest came out with their light and went right back into the earth.

I was so excited and asked them if they could see the light. This was the first time that I had saw light come from trees like that and help a person to release their sickness, or pain. The man that I was working on said that he did not see anything but felt relief throughout his chest and body and felt light.

TWELVE

₪ Ceremonies for Healing

"Ceremonies ae a vital part of life. They have existed for thousands and maybe millions of years. Ceremonies, rituals, or rites of passage's were created to maintain balance in our everyday lives. They were formed to assist us from one stage of our life to the next. They were shaped to carry on a way of showing respect to the elements throughout the different seasons to make sure the harvest and crops grow each year."

"When there is an imbalance in nature, there is an in balance in humanity. It is our role as two-leggeds to honor and respect the planet that we dwell on and all of life's creation that is here for us. All of life's creation includes the food, the water, the sun, the stars, the moon, the trees, and all of the things that we utilize to survive."

~ Crystal D. Gingras ~

First I want to explain how I perceive the labels given to teachers, shamans, and human helpers who lead and assist in ceremonies and healing. A shaman is a person who is learning to live their life studying the herbs (medicine people) and helping to heal themselves and others through the ingestion of tea, smoke, or their physical or spiritual presence. A holy-man is a person who does not use all the herbs, but works primarily through the spirits and the energy of herbs and healing in the Spirit World.

Both the shaman and the holy-person are not powerful themselves, yet they are called a *hollow bone* or an *empty vessel* to be of assistance for the spirits and guides. A spiritual leader is occasionally also called a community leader. Spiritual leaders commonly possess a good-hearted nature and feel as if they are in service for the people and have a basic understanding of the spiritual world. You will typically find such leaders doing acts of kindness, being loving, compassionate, and giving with an open-heart. A chief is an important person who brings wisdom and understanding to the people and is the decision-maker for their tribe or community. Chiefs are now more commonly called presidents and have their own councils within the tribes in North America.

My Great Grandfather, Chief Shunatona, called the presidents or leaders, White Chiefs in his Skookum's Laugh Medicine book. My Great Grandfather is the one who teaches me laughter and humor and how important it is to have this, even in sacred ceremonies. I grew up around so many different elders that seemed to always be serious or straight-faced during a ceremony, and so I took on that role for many years. I would even be upset at the "clown spirits" that were there to help bring humor to the ceremony, because I thought they were "bad". I am honored that his spirit surrounds me with his love and compassion. I will share some one or two of his stories from his book in the last chapter about tools for healing, because humor is very important tool.

The leader, chief, or spiritual leader has a lot to do with the healings and knowledge that is being channeled through them for all of the people in the particular ceremony or ritual. It is a good idea to be acquainted with the shaman or spiritual teacher before they work on you or direct a ceremony for you. Medicine people are also recognized as shamans, but medicine people are not only humans, they are also plant people, tree people, water people, little people, guides, spirits, and ancestors. A large number of the ancient ceremonies were taken away by the settlers hundreds of years ago because they wanted everyone to live like they were accustomed. The indigenous tribes of the United States were not the only ones who had human sacrificial ceremonies; these were practiced all over the world. I have read online that in recent centuries human sacrifices were deemed in-just and stopped. The Pawnee, which is one of my tribes on my mother's side, now have over six-thousand members once again, but not full-bloods. There are only a few full-bloods left, including a couple of my relatives in Pawnee, OK. We are one of the few tribes that practice our ancient feasting ceremony and sacred dance for our people. In Pawnee, we also have one of the last standing sacred round-houses where we do our traditional dances a couple times a year. Nearby, our nation dances with the Osage nation during their sacred dances in the summer as well. These sacred ceremonies are different from pow-wows where anyone can watch and people sell items like a market place. The other difference is that people at pow-wows will contest for the best dancers, outfit and win money.

When I was younger, I used to dance at pow-wows sometimes and I contested one time in Manhattan, but never placed any prizes. A year later, I decided to run for princess for the Warriors Society in Wichita because a man that was substituting for my father was one of the members of the Warriors Society. I did not win that year, however I saw a side of the politics that I did not want to be a part of. I have always had an appreciation for the old respected ways where the dancers are not all flashy, but they are there to honor the earth and their families instead. When I went to the Osage reservation and saw the dances I was honored to be able to watch and assist with serving the food and cleaning dishes for meals. I was also able to help cut up a buffalo and see how they cook outside and make deer jerky outside. I enjoyed working around the Osage dances for three summers and met many of my relatives that I never knew. It wasn't even until I was in my late twenties that I learned about the pow-wows and our sacred dances.

We are now working on harvesting our sacred corn on our reservation and other places in Nebraska where my people used to live on the earth. There are different helpers who help to grow either blue corn, red corn, or what we call eagle corn because it looks like there is a purple eagle on a light-yellow kernel. There are also beans and squash that are grown with the corn, but only one corn may be planted in a yard. You have to be careful to not cross-pollinate the corn to keep it pure. This year was the first year that I was asked to help, and I have much to learn and remember from my elders and ancestors. When I was asked to help, I was in Pawnee for one of my cousin's funerals. He served this country in the army like many of my relatives and ancestors have. He passed away in April of 2010, and I ended up moving to Pawnee a couple of months later.

I worked to build a new community garden near our college on the reservation as well as helping out at a house with the Seed Preservation Project. Although it was emotionally hard on me to be there, I was honored to help out. I was able to attend ceremonies that I would have never heard about and I met many new people and learned a lot about my history.

"Tirawa (also called Atius Tirawa) was the creator god. He taught the Pawnee tattooing, fire-building, hunting, speech and clothing, religious rituals (including the use of tobacco and sacred bundles), and sacrifices. He was associated with the most natural phenomena, including stars and planets, wind, lightening, rain, and thunder. The solar and lunar deities were Shakuru and Pah, respectively. Four major stars were said to represent gods and were part of the creation story, in which the first human being was a girl. The Morning Star and Evening Star mated to create her. Archeologists and anthropologists have determined the Pawnee had a sophisticated understanding of the movement of stars. They noted the nonconforming movements of both Venus (Evening Star) and Mars (Morning Star). The Pawnee centered all aspects of daily life on this celestial observation, including the important cultivation cycle for sacred corn."

"Through both the historical and archaeological record, it is clear that the Pawnee lifestyle was centered on the observation of the celestial bodies, whose movements formed the basis of their seasonal rituals. The positions and construction of their lodges placed their daily life in the center of a scaled-down universe. They could observe the greater universe outside and be reminded of their role in perpetuating the universe. According to one Skidi band Pawnee man at the beginning of the twentieth century, "The Skidi was organized by the stars; these powers above made them into families and villages and taught them how to live and how to perform their ceremonies. The shrines of the four leading villages were given by the four leading stars and represent those stars which guide and rule the people. The Pawnee paid close attention to the universe and believed that for the universe to continue functioning, they had to perform regular ceremonies. These ceremonies were performed before major events, such as semi-annual buffalo hunts, as well as before many other important activities of the year, such as sowing seeds in the spring and harvesting in the fall. The most important ceremony of the Pawnee culture, the Spring Awakening ceremony, was meant to awaken the earth and ready it for planting. It can be tied directly to the celestial bodies." (1)

Healing Ceremony

Healing ceremonies are different in each culture, nations, or tribes. From what I have experienced, they can involve many different kinds of medicine, including tobacco, sage, and cedar. Sometimes the ceremonies are inside of a sweat lodge, or an earth lodge in the Medicine person's home. There is generally more than one medicine person for each tribe, and in my tribe, the Pawnee, there were many medicine people before our people were moved to the reservation in Pawnee. Even then, we had some people practice, but over time it has become much hidden for protection. A lot of ceremonies and old ways must be kept hidden or private to keep them alive.

In healing ceremonies, the person leading the ceremony or performing the extraction of pain or disease has to be prepared and have a lot of experience. Being a medicine person can be a dangerous position as you have to be clear as well as know what to do with the pain that is extracted from the person's body. I have read most of Fools Crow's book on how he practiced some release. He had used a piece of meat for one of his healings. Some medicine people will suck the wound right from the physical body and expose of it. A good example of healing would be the movie <u>The Green</u>

<u>Mile</u> where the man is trying to save the children's lives, and then later he healed a man's urinary tract infection. The part where he "helped" the cancer out for the man's wife was where he got very sick because he couldn't transfer the negative energy out of himself fast enough. This was just a movie, but a great example of what happens to many healers who are not clear enough at the time of healing to transfer energy.

The most important ceremony that I have ever practiced is the ceremony of giving thanks. Giving gratitude is one of the most important parts of living and surviving here on earth. From time to time, we may become selfish and greedy and forget where we came from. By giving gratitude each day, we remember that what we have is very precious. It is taking the time to give gratitude each day for what you experienced in that day and for what will surely be there tomorrow. If you ate food from the earth, then give thanks to the earth and all the elements for growing and nurturing that food so that you can survive. How about the trees? Each tree supplies life to four people. If there were no trees, we would not exist. We all co-exist together and literally would not survive without each other.

When I bless my food, I place my hands over my food to fill it with love and gratitude for the earth, the sun, the water, the air, the fire, and all of the people that helped to plant it and grow it. Eating is a very special ceremony which can spread many prayers, love, forgiveness, and powerful healing. Taking time to give gratitude to your food will improve your health and quality of your life. Thank you to the plant people, the animal kingdom, the ones that swim, fly, and even the creepy-crawlers; we need all of them to survive.

I also want to express the importance of wanting to be a medicine person, as this takes many, many years to practice and learn and is not an easy task, nor is a path for everyone. Usually, a parent or elder will pass down their teachings and abilities to their relatives. Here is just a little bit of history on the Pawnees.

"Pawnee priests were known for their magic, and many ceremonies continued to be practiced until the 1920s before they died under the pressure of missionaries and government officials who wanted to destroy the ancient Pawnee traditions. Priests played an important part in Pawnee culture, with elaborate ceremonies performed before every important event. The Doctor Dance, Scalp Dance, Victory Dance, Corn Dance, Water Dance, and Ghost Dance were some of the more important ceremonies. Seven singers were required for the Ghost Dance, which lasted for four days and four nights. The Doctor Dance was performed periodically to heal people and to demonstrate the magical powers of the doctors.

One of the most important was the Pipe Dance, which symbolized the rebirth of the tribe. In the dance, the pipe symbolized man's contact with God, and the singer offered prayers to God through the pipe. Myra Lone Chief Eppler, who was born on July 15, 1894, became one of the major factors in preserving ancient Pawnee traditions. Having participated in many of the tribal ceremonies, especially those reserved for children of chiefs, in her later years she became a valuable resource for ethnologists and historians attempting to preserve a traditional Pawnee culture that almost disappeared." (2) Now, here I am, living on my reservation in Pawnee to help with our Pawnee Seed Preservation Project, and I wish I knew our sacred Corn Dance ceremony!

Another ceremony that has become a part of my life is the Ayahuasca ceremony. The mother, or some people have called Ayahuasca grandmother, is a great healer for many different ailments. I have heard of people that get healing for the mind, addictions, ego, anger, and cancer. There are a lot of people that travel to other countries to participate in this ceremony, and there are also teachers who bring the medicine to the states to share with other people here.

I participated for the first time two years ago and had an amazing experience. It only took about twenty minutes for the medicine to "kick in," and then about an hour later, it "kicked out" and along with it, any blocks I had in my body, mind, and energy. At first, my ego kicked in when I saw the lights shoot up through my body and align my energies. I thought to myself, "Duh," I know how to do that." It was as if all of the memories of the many lifetimes I had before with the medicine were right there with me again. I noticed that there were a lot of other spirits in the room, some which were alive in other countries, and just there to "help."

What I have noticed in some ceremonies is that the medicine people are competitive or want to be the best. I say be the best you can be by helping with honor, respect, and humility for other healers and all people involved. I explained how the ego and obnoxiousness were not welcome here; only love was. I explained how there is a time and place for horseplay, and this wasn't the place. It's funny how when you're in ceremony and your inner child comes out to play, but the elder spirits say, "Hey, go sit down." That just makes me smile on the inside.

I don't remember if I sang at this first ceremony, but I think I did. I was always ready to help and wanted to make sure it was right with the person leading the ceremony. When I am in Sweat Lodge, we all sing together. At a healing ceremony I participated in a teepee, we all sang together as well. It was the third time that I did ceremony and sang that I actually had a pretty amazing spiritual experience where my mind was clear enough for the spirits actually to sing through me while the leader was blowing smoke on the participants for healing. I remember having my hands held palm up and my fingers started moving fast, one by one. With each finger, a different octave would come bellowing out and sometimes with a different voice. I could feel the waves of light emerging from the vibrations of my voice to all of the people in the room. There was one voice that was actually my friend's voice that was blowing smoke on the participants for healing at the time.

After the ceremony was over, I remember one of my friends there telling me that they heard him singing through me. That was the second experience that I had with channeling other healing energy in a ceremony. I believe if you are interested in this ceremony and have not tried it yet, you should find a safe place to have this ceremony. It is important to have a teacher and practice in a respectful way, as it is for all ceremonies and medicine.

Another ceremony that I have learned is the blessing the water ceremony. There are many different ways to bless the water, and I will share this simple, yet powerful one that each of you can practice and share with others. First of all, blessing the water each time before you drink will connect you with the water that is all around you and inside of you. You simply rub your hands together a bit to build up a little energy and then place your hands over your water for about five or ten seconds. You may wish to think love or balance, peace or health while blessing your water. If you are at home or alone, then you can say this out loud. The actual vibration of your voice saying that word will help to infuse the water with what you say.

Each time that you practice this blessing the water ceremony, you are also blessing and aligning yourself. This can be practiced in a body of water outside, in the shower, in the bath, or with a bowl of water in front of you. First, you take three to five deep breaths and cleanse your energy and relax the mind. Next, face your right palm upwards and say, "This left hand represents the grandmother water spirits." Then, face your right palm up and say, "This right hand represents the grandfather water spirits." After you say both out loud, scoop up a handful of water and say, "I now thank and bless the grandmother and grandfather water spirits and connect you both together in peace and balance." If you would like to add a special blessing for yourself, then scoop a second cup of water in your palms and ask for special blessings from the grandmother and grandfather water spirits of life. When you are finished, make sure that you give thanks to the water and the ceremony and for all things in your day that you had to give thanks for.

"Ya-we-ya-hey, Heya, hey-hiya.

Ya-we-ya-hey, Heya-hey-hiya,

Ya-we-yah-heya, Hey, Yo-Hey."

(Repeat two or three times)

One of my favorite chants to sing in the morning, at night, and when I offer my food to the ancestors, helpers, guides, and the Creator.

The Inipi ceremony is known as a sweat lodge ceremony and is now practiced throughout the world. The Inipi is the Lakota word for sweat lodge, although many other tribes practice this cleansing ritual for the mind, body and spirit as well. Out of the million tribes that still exist, there are hundreds of different tribes that practice this ceremony as well as in other countries throughout the world including England, Ireland, Guatemala, and Australia to name a few. Recently in lodge, I heard one of the elders saying that you must to your four years of vision quest with four days and five nights, as well as speak the Lakota language so that the ancestors will understand you. My belief is that we are all related and that any language you speak, no matter where you are, the Creator will understand you. I know that, just because I do not speak Pawnee, my ancestors, the stars and my relatives can still hear me, even when I sing prayer songs in Lakota. The ancestors listen from your heart and spirit through the vibrations of your voice, not from your mind and language. Your mind and body are only temporary here, while your spirit and soul are what you are in this lifetime, the past, and future lifetimes.

Some say, the Inipi ceremony was brought here over a thousand years ago from the White Buffalo Calf Woman who came with a chanupa and shared these ways with the Lakota people. The chanupa is a sacred pipe, and some elders and natives may find it disrespectful to call a chanupa a pipe. It is *wakan*, which means sacred in Lakota to their people as well as many other people who carry them. From what I have learned, if you carry a chanupa, then you have decided to walk the Red Road and be of service for your people. That means when you see something or someone that needs help and they ask for help, then you do your best to help them. You refrain from alcohol and drugs and from doing or speaking anything that can cause harm to yourself or another person. Sometimes, people may decide to drink and do other things on earth, so they put the chanupa away for a few years until they are ready again, or pass it along to someone else. The Red Road is a ceremony called life.

Two years ago, in 2008, I attended a hanblecheyapi ceremony, or a vision quest. Some may call it a fast for one to three days. My first one I did one night and came back in the morning. It started with a cleansing ceremony in the sweat lodge; then when I came back in the morning, I went right back into the lodge. This is how it is every time that I have gone. You have a supporter who waits with the elder or person who is leading it. The job of that support person is very important because they are praying for you and helping to keep you strong. They are able to drink water and have meals, and while you are praying, you go without.

I would like to share this sacred vision that gave me the support and the drive to travel to Pine Ridge, South Dakota, for the last two years. My first day I was sitting there praying and connecting to the huge tree that was across the creek from where I was sitting, and I sang songs all day and prayed all night, and admittingly I fell asleep for awhile. The next day I kept praying, and the heat was making me sweat; I kept praying, and that evening I fell asleep again. When I awoke from that last sleep, I remember being in an Inipi ceremony, and there were about four different elders in there: one was from India, one was from Tibet, one was Native American, and the other I do not remember. When I arrived back at home, I decided to check my emails. I immediately noticed an email from the same night of my vision, so I opened it. It was information about helping to build natural homes for Pine Ridge, South Dakota.

For years I had dreams of lodges being in people's back yards all over a city. I would see people meditating all over in the yards with their backs against the trees. They were all sitting straight up so the trees could connect energies with them to help cleanse and renew their energy. I would be driving or flying around all over and see them sitting everywhere! These round homes that I saw I thought were sweat lodges; then when I saw this picture of the earth ship home, I realized that's what I had been "seeing"!

Since I was one years old, I have attended inipi (sweat lodge) ceremonies with my mother and some of my other teachers and tribes throughout North America. Looking at this email right after my vision, I knew that South Dakota was calling me. I knew it was finally time to travel there. Most of all, I was finally shown myself that it's time for our elders from different countries to come together.

About ten years ago several of my teachers here in Turtle Island met with the indigenous teachers from South America, and they shared different knowledge which was shared with me. I know that many different people have been traveling for many years to learn and follow their hearts. It's time for us on a much wider scale to learn and to grow and stop being afraid and living in our separateness. We have only suffered from being separate, not just separate from ourselves and from each other, but separate from the trees, the plants, and the vines. They are asking us to come back and connect with them again.

My first experience with Ayahuasca was in 2009. I wasn't sure about attending the ceremony as the only thing I heard about it was from the elders from Wisdom Keepers. I had heard that one of the elders asked for a second cup of tea right away, and soon her spirit was in her daughter's house. She had to hide, so she wouldn't scare anyone. I knew that it was for special healing and that it will make you purge, literally. I wasn't sure about the hallucinogenic involved and had only practiced talking to spirits by fasting and prayer. The medicine that you drink has a plant that contains DMT which causes you to see in colors or other pictures that you would not normally see. I talked with some of my friends about it and decided to wait for a year to make sure it was the right choice for me.

I ended up meeting someone that I felt comfortable with to attend the ceremony together. She attended Ayahuasca ceremony in Peru before and highly recommended it for me. The teacher arrived in the states along with several other people and some friends that I had invited over. We all had our area picked out with a little chair, blanket to keep warm, and the puke bucket. We also had some bottled water and either tissue paper or toilet paper. One of my friends recommended a diaper, but I opted out on that one (It's been four ceremonies now, and I still haven't had that problem).

The ceremony started at sundown with the leader blowing smoke to protect the space that we were in. He made a beautiful altar and had lots of special instruments to help with the ceremony. He had been practicing for over ten years, and my friend who invited me has been going for all those years. I was very comfortable, and the ceremony was very relaxed and powerful. I do think that it is very important to know who is leading and make sure that you are in a sacred space. This medicine is very sacred and needs to be respected as such. If you do decide that this is a path for you, then please make sure that you are under supervision of a leader, shaman, or someone who works in the spirit world.

CHAPTER THIRTEEN

₪ Tools as Medicine

"This is my song that was given to me from Spirit during ceremony in New Mexico. This is a song that was given to me to share to connect our hearts together as one. I play this song to cleanse the water that runs through our veins, which is the same water that runs through the Mother Earth. I share this song with you, and it is my honor. I share this song because this is how I practice my medicine."

~Crystal D. Gingras~

The sound that the voice carries is one of the most beautiful and powerful tools that we have. When you are born, you make your call; you make your cry that you are here and you let your relatives know. When you cry for help, your ancestors and guides hear you; they hear your powerful voice, and they listen to your pure heart. We all have our own voice, and that is a tool that we always carry with us, no matter where we go. Our bodies are our instruments, and it is up to us to keep them tuned and in good shape to be able to utilize them when we need them. It is time to find your voice, to find your song, and sing it. And, when you are ready, share it with who the Creator sends to you for assistance.

Here is the song that was given to me:

"Yá-ni leche lo- Hey, Yá-ni leche lo- Hey,

Yá-ni Wàkondashe Hey Yá Hi Yo-,Yá-ni Wàkondashe Hey Yá Hi Yo,

Yá-ni leche lo- Hey, Yá-ni leche lo- Hey,

Yá-ni Wàkondashe Hey Yá Hi Yo-,Yá-ni Wàkondashe Hey Yá Hi Yo,

Wey-ya Hi-yo Hey, Hay-ya Hi-yo,

Wey-ya Hi-yo Hey, Hay-ya Hi-yo."

A common thing that I see with people that are beginning on their path is they are afraid to sing or do "sound healing." Relative, if this includes you, please allow yourself to accept that sound healing, or whatever label you have been taught; is your birthright. When I say "birthright," I mean that each of us was born with our voice, and this sound healing, some say, was the very beginning of Creation itself. So, please begin to trust yourself and sing and chant away!

While you are singing and practicing sharing your voice, musical instruments are very complementary. I grew up to the sound of drums beating inside the heated, safe lodge where my heart was pounding from my chest. Every breath I took was cleansing out my insides and the beat of the drum took me deeper into myself than I will ever understand. I loved being in ceremony, and to this day, it's still my favorite place to be. Some songs would be sung with rattles that would help to awaken and transform different parts of your body and spirit. Not only were the drums and rattles helping to balance out certain parts of me, but the rhythms in which they were played as well.

Instruments have been known to be applied for healing tools since they were made. One of the most popular healing instruments of all times is the harp. There are so many statues of the angel that holds and plays the harp. People who play harps will play them for hospitals and ill children or for people dying. The string instruments are said to be very healing for the heart and help to ease the pain and suffering in the mind and the physical body. For me, just being in the presence of a harp is very calming. The closest I have come to a string instrument is playing the viola in middle school and now I have a guitar that sits in my home waiting for me to put into practice.

Tools are essentially everywhere, but they work the best when you can relate to them. Often times they are a hobby or an interest that you have in something. Tools can be your favorite colors or symbols that you are attracted to. They can be many other things besides instruments. The most extensive tool is your imagination. Other tools that are free and readily accessible are hand and body movements and placements, the breath and the eyes. Basically, everything can be applied as a tool.

When I lived in Topeka, KS in the year of 2000, I was gifted with my first medicine bag from a good friend of mine, Donny. It was passed down to him from a man that shared with him his sacred medicine. The bag was represented by a turtle on one side of the leather, and by a medicine shield with tribal designs on the other side. I wore that bag for many years around my neck before it fell apart. The green and orange beads were beginning to wear on it, and the leather was getting old from all the wear. I wore it in my showers, in the sweat lodges, and beneath my shirt next to my heart. Then, about five years later, my mother hand-made a leather medicine bag for me with a turtle beaded on it that I still have today. It was large enough to place my other medicine bag in along with medicine that I use.

I am often asked by people that see my medicine bag what I carry inside. I think that anyone who feels that they need a medicine bag can receive one. I will also share what is in my medicine bag with someone who is genuinely asking me and not just asking just because. I sometimes share this medicine with other people in ceremony, or I use it when someone is sick. The first time that I left my medicine bag at home was when I traveled to Guatemala. For a long time, I felt like my medicine bag protected me from harm, and that I had to have it with me at all times. Because this journey to Guatemala was for my own healing, and a huge transformation in my life, I wanted to be open to the unknown and welcome in new medicine and tools.

By the end of the trip I had receive a beautiful red bean necklace and bracelet that was made specifically for protection. And, I just now remembered at the beginning of my journey while I was in L.A., a man at the tea shop I went to gave me a small stone for protection as well. Besides all of the stones, crystals, beads, beans, and amulets, there are always the non-visible, spiritual forms of healing and protection such as calling on the angels, practicing Reiki and breath-work.

Since 1992 I have been studying Reiki and in my studies of Reiki healing I learned that Reiki is composed of the breath, touch, tapping, massaging, the eyes, visualizing symbols, chanting symbols and hand placements. After I became a Reiki Master in 1996, I wanted to teach Reiki to others and utilize this form of healing to help with cancer, arthritis, and all physical and emotional suffering. If you research Reiki, you find that there are many different tools that people utilize with Reiki and even teach courses about them. Some that I am familiar with are Reiki Drumming and Reiki Crystals. The Reiki symbols will be applied via the imagination over the surface of the drum, or inside of the drum, so that when the drum is played, it will create the particular healing effect of the symbol. If crystals are being utilized for a tool with Reiki, then you can place the crystal in between your hands while you visualize the symbol being inserted into the crystal. It is good to do this with a quartz crystal if you are a

Reiki practitioner.

If you are working with crystals from the earth, then you want to make sure that if you didn't dig them up yourself, that you cleanse them before you work with them. Since crystals come from the earth, you can simply place them back in the ground with the intention to be cleansed for one to three days. Another way that you can cleanse them or charge them is in the moonlight, or with sage, cedar or Epsom salts. I shared about cleansing with sage in chapter ten when I shared about the sacred plants and vines as medicine.

As I covered earlier in the four directions, animals and elements are also very good tools to apply in your life. Different cultures see different colors and animals as sacred and are recognized in particular areas or around the world. Oftentimes businesses will use different symbols to market their company. I have noticed that some of the symbols used today at coffee shops and consumer stores are thousands of years old. I enjoy collecting old symbol books and then look up all of the symbols that companies use across the globe. What I noticed is a lot of car companies that use ancient emblems on the back or front of cars. You never know what it made on purpose for marketing, and what is done on "accident", but it's always interesting for me to look up the meanings.

The most common tools that are practiced among all cultures that I have seen are drums, water, bells, and chants or songs. Tools may be also viewed as a sacred space or alter that is created. Within that sacred space or tool, are many different tools put together to create a specific need for that person, family or business. One of my favorite sounds was a man chanting sacred sounds while he repeatedly sounded the large flat bronze gong. It was at this place that I also ate some of the most wonderful food, which reminds me how powerful food is in assisting us on our journey.

Many people that I do ceremony with will eat specific foods for preparing their mind and body for ceremony or a particular endeavor. A huge part of being able to apply food as a tool is about knowing what plants and foods are good for particular areas in the body. For example, if you are doing a ceremony for a cleansing of the mind, then you can eat foods that support your brain such as walnuts, fish and almonds. Perhaps you are doing a ceremony for cleansing the body, and you can eat lighter foods such as salads, oranges, apples, and plenty of water.

The more that you decide to practice with tools or attend ceremonies and continue learning about yourself and the earth, you will find that there are many tools that you enjoy playing with that work great for you. A great way to begin to find the tools that work for you are to apply one of your inner tools, your imagination, and see what thoughts are created when you ask which tools work the best for you. You can ask yourself by asking out loud, "What tools can I utilize for my highest good for _____?" You can fill in the blank with whatever specific reason you need a tool in your life. This can be for healing, happiness, for growth, for insight on your goals, your life purpose, love, travel, paying bills, school, my relationship, my children and anything that you need assistance or guidance with at this time. Learn to trust your intuition by practicing and applying what comes to your mind as you ask this question. Your practice and experiences are going to be your greatest teachers in this lifetime, but you will not learn if you don't try, and you know your growing good when you can begin to laugh at your own mistakes.

If you ever feel that you are around a teacher that tells you what to use and what is right or wrong for you, then you might want to reconsider another teacher. We are ALL teachers and students, so please try not to be so hard on yourself. Always follow what your intuition and heart says and not what someone else tells you. Even if it appears to come with love and respect, your most important things to listen to and follow are your own intuition and instincts. Remember, you are born love, and no one is higher or lower than you. Good luck on your journey and all of my love, from my heart, to your heart.

Crystal D. Gingras

"Respect all of life, and the experiences one has gone through to become the person they are today."

CHIEF JOE SHUNATONA

As promised earlier in the book, here are some stories from my Great Grandfather Chief Shunatona, creator of SKOOKUM, "the dumb Indian." But first, I want to introduce you to him as he is introduced in his book. "This book is America's foremost exponent of Indian humor and the greatest showman who ever descended from the ORIGINAL AMERICANS.

He is a full-blooded Pawnee-Otoe with a background of experience the professional entertainment world beyond compare.

As Master of Ceremonies, he has emceed deluxe theatrical presentations in theatres from coast to coast and has been a headliner on all the major circuits in this country and Europe. He has consistently brought honor to the Indian race in the field of motion pictures, radio, stage and television. His incomparable characterization of SKOOKUM originated in the Orpheum Theater in Seattle, Washington, when a group of Indians called him, "Skookum," which means "good." He has participated in all the annual pow-wows of Oklahoma such as the Pawnee Homecoming, the American Indian Exposition at Anadarko, the Ponca Pow-Wow, the Osage dances at Pawhuska, and has been the official announcer for the Gallup Ceremonials." Chief Shunatona studied in the field of fine arts and is well known as a musical maestro. He enjoys the distinction of having played for two Presidential Inaugural Balls in Washington. In addition, he is a writer, director, producer, and actor. His talents fit any occasion, from entertainment in school auditoriums to giant open-air spectacles."

GREETINGS FROM SKOOKUM

"Boy Howdy, already 50 years pass since Oklahoma became civilize and Teddy Roosevelt he bring it to United States.

Long time 'go used to could hunt and fish an' shore live it the happy life. Ride horses, raise pumpkins, corn, squash, an' Great Spirit He give it to us all kinds huckle berries, wild strawberries, black berries, an' lots things. Anytime, could stop under a tree or open prairie an' talk to Great Spirit' an' give thanks. Now days have to wait til Sunday, put-em-on necktie an' shine-em-up shoes an' try to look "keen" before go church.

I guess that's what you call civilize! Spoil-em hunting grounds an' fence-em-up land an' build big fat tall teepees in Tulsa an' Oklahoma City an' lots places. Big smoke comin' out factories looks like he says all time, "money money money." So much money, Now Uncle Sam he says "tax tax tax" an' if you don't pay it he goin" give you free taxi ride, too.

Oklahoma he do that in jus" 50 years. But all right, I guess, cause Big Chiefs lawmakers most of it Injuns. Head man boss he's Governor Gary. An' we got Bob Kerr, Mike Monroney, Ed Edmondson, an' Whip Man Carl Albert; all good ones Oklahoma Injuns. Page Belcher over here, too, but he's Republican tribe, I think.

Injuns goin' celebrate plenty much this year with lots pow-wows, cause we don't care, even 50 years civilize we still got it much more Injuns than used to was. Some got plenty smart in their heads, too. Cherokee "Nap" Johnson, he's Supreme Court Judge; Allie Reynolds, big New York Yankee Doodle he's Creek tribe; Y'ever seen Maria Tallchief dance? She's Osage. An' Bill Keeler, head man Phillips Petroleum Company, he's Cherokee Chief, too. Lots Injuns we got over here; lawyers, judges, teachers, all kinds ball players, artists, music mans, an' Generals, Majors, Captains, Gee Whizz, we got those kind in Army an' Navy! Two Injuns got Congress Medal of Honor, too, Choctaw Jack Montgomery and Creek Ernest Childers. An' Washin'ton Hall of Fame we got two more Injuns, Sequoyah and Bill Rogers, purty good Cherokees. Me, I shore like it all these Injuns.

I guess Injuns he can stand this civilize all right. So we goin' celebrate good this year. Don't have to fire-water, neither. Jus' look toward the Heavan an' thank Great Spirit for eff'rything, more much cause we understand pale-face kind civilize little bit.

Maybeso next time when 50 years come again, me, I lose em plenty tooth an' when rainy weather my knees hurt, but even my hands shaky I gonna make sign language, "OKLAHOMA* GOOD LAND* ME, I LIVE HERE* GLAD* OKLAHOMA, LAND OF RED MAN!" How!"

I really wish I could have been alive with my Great Grandfather, but his spirit brings me smiles and good feelings. This joke I want to share is called "Dumb Skookum", and it's my favorite joke that I share as often as possible with people to make them smile.

DUMB SKOOKUM

"I don't gone school, that's why kinda dumb-bell I guess. All I learn it is A and B and C. An' I guess school teacher he's got lots more, don't it? When big war time come Uncle Sam he made ABC everything.

One day doctor man he said, "Skookum, you okay now, guess may-beso you go army camp." So I went army camp, and head boss, he said, "Skookum, you go Company D" – an' Gee Whizz, I couldn't find that Company D no-where cause all I knowed was A-B-C.

HOW MANY HORSES?

"When an Indian went to the bank for a loan the banker insisted that he mortgage his horses for the loan. When it was all explained to the Indian he agreed to leave his horses for security. Not long afterward the Indian received an oil royalty check of considerable size and went to the bank to pay his loan. The banker took out what was necessary and on giving the Indian what was left, said, "John, that is a lot of money to be carrying around; someone might rob you or even try to kill you if they know you have all that money. Why dont you let me keep it for you in my bank?"

"The Indian considered very seriously for a few seconds, then said, "How many horses YOU got?"

BIG SHOT COUNCILMAN

"I jus' come back Washin'ton, he's sure big one, don't it? I sawn it big house where Uncle Sam he shore try to smart aleck, Jus' stick-it-up his feet on desk an' smoke-em his big cigar, and he sed, "Skookum, what's matter you?" So I said it, "Uncle Sam, I shore don't like-it how you treat-em Injuns. I'm going to sed it somethin' right now an' I'm not goin' sed it on you behind either, I'm goin' sed it right to you face.

What for you close-em-up Injun hospitals an' some Injun Agency? You shore like to shut-em up them agency an' hospitals an' save-em lots money. Then you ship it all over to old country. That kind way I don't like it.

An' long time 'go you made-em treaty with Injuns. All Injuns you goin' give it 160 acres land. Injuns he think looks like purty good, maybeso,--so he stick-it-on there his thumb print. But Gee Whizz, land it's no good worth dam. Jus' lots rocks an' cant grow nothin' beans. An more worse oil it's come out an' dirty it up all my land.

Some-one he beat-em Injun out his land; build-em big towns like Tulsa, Muskogee, and lots of em. Then you collect it that Income tax. Ef-fery year you collect it that tax. White man he sed it we don't wanna pay them tax, maybeso more better we give land back to Injuns! But Injuns don't want it now!"

That's what I sed it to Uncle Sam. Me, I don't talk much but when I sed somethin' I mean it.

I sed it, "Uncle Sam, when you sed-it somethin' and sign-it-up those treaty I want you to mean it. An' I want you to did it what you sed you was gonna done it!" (3)

BIBLIOGRAPHY

(1) http://en.wikipedia.org/Pawnee_mythology

(2) *Pawnee Pride*, Kenny A. Franks and Paul F. Lambert. 1994: Oklahoma Heritage Association

(3) *Skookum's Laugh Medicine*, By Chief Joe Shunatona. 1957

(*) *The Hako*, Alice C. Fletcher 1996: University of Nebraska Press. The Hako was originally published in 1904.

ABOUT THE AUTHOR

Crystal D. Gingras was born on May 18, 1980 when Mt. St. Helen's erupted. Her mother named her Crystal after the crystals that form inside the earth from the lavas heat. Crystal's mother, Sue Shunatona is from the Pawnee Nation. As well as Otoe and Wyandotte. Her father is an enrolled member of the Flathead Nation (Confederated Salish and Kootenai- S'elish Ktunaxa). Crystal was born in Wichita, KS and then moved around all of her childhood with her mother and older sister, and later, two brothers Nesahdo and Jason. She also has over ten brothers and sisters on her father's side.

Crystal's childhood consisted of indigenous ceremonies from the Apache Nation, Lakota Nation and other indigenous peoples of the United States with her mother. Before the age of ten she enjoyed helping spirits cross over to the other side with their families and loved helping with the sacred fires for ceremonies.

I am very fortunate to have many different teachers from all walks of life and I am proud to have had the opportunities to study meditations from India, Nepal, Tibet, as well as indigenous people of the land where I was born. I was blessed to see His Holiness the 14th Dalai

Lama in 2007 and travel outside of the states to Guatemala and Egypt. I am very honored to have chosen a mother so loving and open to all walks of life. She has shown me the true meaning of Mitakuye Oyasin, "We Are All Related".

Index

Made in the USA
Lexington, KY
15 November 2018